University of Cambridge Department of Applied Economics

OCCASIONAL PAPER 42

THE STEEL INDUSTRY

International Comparisons of Industrial Structure and Performance

The Steel Industry

International Comparisons of
Industrial Structure and Performance

ANTHONY COCKERILL
in collaboration with
AUBREY SILBERSTON

CAMBRIDGE UNIVERSITY PRESS

Published by the Syndics of the Cambridge University Press
Bentley House, 200 Euston Road, London NW1 2DB
American Branch: 32 East 57th Street, New York, N.Y. 10022

© Department of Applied Economics, University of Cambridge 1974

ISBN: 0 521 09878 5

First published 1974

Typeset by EWC Wilkins Ltd, London N12 OEH and printed in Great Britain
by Alden & Mowbray Ltd at the Alden Press, Oxford

TO JANET

Contents

List of Tables

List of Appendices

Preface

This paper embodies the results of Anthony Cockerill's work on international comparisons of structure and performance in the steel industry. The work was carried out at the Department of Applied Economics under my general supervision, but to Anthony Cockerill must go the credit for assembling and analysing relevant data from a very large number of different sources. The paper almost certainly represents the most complete collection of information yet available bearing on the main object of our research – an assessment of differences in efficiency in the same industry in a number of countries, and an attempt to explain these, bearing in mind particularly differences in industrial structure and in scale of production. Even so, it was easier to produce the data given here which relate to structure, and the estimates of the economies theoretically associated with large scale, than it was to devise useful measures of differences in efficiency, and to try to explain these differences – but this of course is inevitable.

The paper has been read by experts in the steel industry and their comments have been embodied as far as possible. They have pointed out that Anthony Cockerill has had to make many assumptions, but they admit that they could not themselves have done much better in providing more accurate data in many of the fields where estimates have been attempted. We would not wish it to be thought therefore that we would stand by every estimate made in this paper, although it is the result of a great deal of careful work. While some of the statistics are inevitably not up-to-date, we hope that the qualitative material takes account of recent developments in the industry.

It is intended that one or more further Occasional Papers on other industries should be published in due course. Work is proceeding on brewing and on man-made fibres.

I should declare a personal interest in the steel industry, as a non-executive board member of the British Steel Corporation. The present study is however in no way connected with my work for the BSC, makes use of no confidential data, and any opinions expressed are those of the principal author and not of the Corporation.

December 1973

Aubrey Silberston
Nuffield College, Oxford

Acknowledgements

The research upon which this report is based is part of a wider study of international variations in industrial structure and performance carried out in the Department of Applied Economics at Cambridge between October 1969 and August 1972. It was financed by an award from the Social Science Research Council, whose support is gratefully acknowledged. Various additional research and secretarial facilities have been provided by Teesside Polytechnic and the University of Salford.

Detailed case-study work of this type relies heavily for its success upon the willing cooperation of a considerable number of commercial organisations. The valuable assistance of the following is most warmly appreciated: The American Iron and Steel Institute; Bethlehem Steel Corporation; The British Steel Corporation; Chambre Syndicale de la Sidérurgie Française; Cockerill, s.a., Comité de la Sidérurgie Belge; Eastern Stainless Steel (Baltimore); Republic Steel Corporation; and the United States Steel Corporation.

The work has been carried out under the general supervision of Aubrey Silberston, now Official Fellow in Economics at Nuffield College, Oxford, who has given me the full benefit of his wide experience and knowledge, both within the general area of industrial economics and with specific regard to the steel industry. I owe a great intellectual debt to Professor F.M. Scherer, currently Senior Research Fellow at the International Institute of Management, Berlin, who solved two tricky methodological obstacles. His contribution will be immediately apparent to anyone reading his *The Economics of Multi-Plant Operation: An International Comparisons Study*, with A. Beckstein, E. Kaufer and R.D. Murphy, (Cambridge, Mass: Harvard University Press) forthcoming.

In the DAE, Mrs. Marion Hughes and her computors have willingly undertaken the bulk of the statistical analysis, and Mrs. Lilian Silk and her typists have produced a stream of high-quality work. Chris Clayton-Smith gave yeoman service with field-work in France in 1971. Finally, my wife has cheerfully suffered the demands which the work has made on my time, as well as producing two delightful children and coping with three moves of house.

I have tried to report accurately and interpret correctly the information I have collected. The responsibility for any errors of omission or commission is solely mine.

Anthony Cockerill
University of Salford

November 1973

I

Introduction

One indisputable fact about the performance of the British economy in the post-war period is that it has grown more slowly than other advanced industrial nations. Measured in terms of the rate of increase of gross national product at constant prices, the British growth rate has (until the last year or so) hovered between annual rates of 2 to 3 per cent, in contrast with the 5 to 6 per cent of France and the Federal Republic of Germany, and the 9 or 10 per cent of Japan. Concern over the British growth rate has reflected the desire to raise living standards at least in line with those elsewhere and to help to eradicate poverty. Only recently has it been tempered by considerations of the costs of growth in terms of damage to the environment and to the 'quality' of life.[1]

The abortive attempts of successive Governments to generate sustained growth by fiscal and monetary means, only to be frustrated by supply constraints, inflation, deterioration in the balance of payments, and (under a fixed exchange rate system) an insupportable draining of the reserves, are well charted.[2] In the mid-1960s considerable attention was directed towards the contribution of the manufacturing sector to economic growth.[3] It was argued that, as compared with the extractive and services sectors, expansion of maufacturing offered the prospect of on-going economies of scale, which would raise efficiency, increase the level of international competitiveness, and hence lay the foundation for further growth. Evidence was presented to show that nations with relatively fast growing manufacturing sectors also had relatively fast increases in productivity, which in turn were strongly associated with relatively fast rates of overall economic growth. The major factor inhibiting the expansion of the manufacturing sector in Britain, it was suggested, was the shortage of labour available, and in 1966 the Selective Employment Tax was introduced to discriminate between labour in the manufacturing and services sectors, one of the objectives of which was the transfer of labour into manufacturing. Associated with this was the suggestion that depreciation of the currency exchange rate would give an initial boost to exports of manufactured goods and thus prime the engine of growth.

Parallel with this line of thought went the (less controversial) notion that the

1 See for example E.J. Mishan, *The Costs of Economic Growth*, (London: Staples) 1967.

2 For example, S. Brittan, *Steering the Economy*, (Harmondsworth: Penguin Press), 1971.

3 N. Kaldor, *Causes of the Slow Rate of Economic Growth of the United Kingdom*, Inaugural Lecture, (Cambridge: Cambridge University Press), 1966.

structure of British industry was in some respects inadequate. Because of historic slow growth, restrictive business practices, monopolistic labour unions and managerial lassitude, the opportunities for rationalisation and the introduction of modern technology had not been taken to the full, and as a result the price and quality of British goods were uncompetitive in world markets. It was suggested that as compared with other leading industrial nations, the overall sizes of plant and firms were too small, product ranges were too diverse (and consequently production runs were too short), and that equipment was obsolete and working practices outdated.

The need to restructure industry was embodied in Government policy in the notion of the 'white hot technological revolution' and the Industrial Reorganisation Corporation was established in 1966 specifically to foster and assist rationalisation through merger. Indeed, during the second half of the 1960s merger activity proceeded at an unprecedented rate, the peak being reached in 1968 when there were 946 mergers with a total asset value of £1,946 million.[1] The Government referred to the Monopolies Commission only a small number of the mergers which satisfied the relevant criteria.[2] Since 1958 the overall level of concentration in manufacturing industry in the UK has increased steadily. It has been argued that between 1958 and 1963 the increase was due to the net effects of three factors, each of approximately equal influence: increases in concentration primarily attributable to mergers, increases in concentration due to differential internal expansion and decreases in concentration.[3] Over the longer period from 1954 to 1965, however, mergers apparently accounted for almost one half of the increase in concentration.[4] At the industry level substantial rises in concentration occured as a result of mergers: for example, between 1958 and 1972 the market share of the leading seven producers in the brewing industry rose from 25 per cent to 80 per cent.[5]

More recently policy has to some extent changed direction. The emphasis has shifted from mergers to competition as a means of raising industrial efficiency. The most important dimension of this policy is, of course, Britain's entry into the European Economic Community as from 1 January 1973, but there is evidence also of a less lenient approach towards mergers between British firms.[6] Exposure to the 'cold shower' of aggressive competition (whether from foreign producers or from other domestic manufacturers), it is argued, will prompt firms to improve their technical efficiency and to tighten their internal or managerial efficiency (often

1 *Financial Times*, 23 November 1972.

2 Following the Mergers and Monopolies Act 1965 these were a market share of one-third or more, or a total value of assets taken over of £5 million or above. In 1973 the market share criterion was reduced to 25 per cent.

3 P.E. Hart, M.A. Utton and G. Walshe, *Mergers and Concentration in British Industry*, National Institute of Economic and Social Research Occasional Papers 26 (Cambridge: Cambridge University Press), 1973, Chapter 3.

4 M.A. Utton, 'The effect of mergers on concentration: UK manufacturing industry, 1954-65', *Journal of Industrial Economics*, November 1971, pp. 42–58.

5 A. Cockerill, 'Mergers and Rationalisation in the Brewing Industry', *The Brewer*, (forthcoming)

6 Sir Geoffrey Howe, 'Government Policy on Mergers', *Trade and Industry*, 31 October 1973.

termed X-efficiency because its source is disparate and uncertain),[1] favouring the growth of the more thrusting and inventive companies. Raising X-efficiency may have more influence upon unit costs than increasing the scale of production.[2] Selective expansion will then allow new investment, the introduction of best-practice techniques of production and consequent rises in the productivity of both labour and capital, which will lay the basis for further growth.

The explanations of poor performance upon which these policies are based suffer, *inter alia*, from a lack of detailed information on the sources and extent of economies of scale (which would permit an assessment of the degree to which these are left unexploited by the prevailing industrial structure); on the degree to which the structure of manufacturing industry in the UK differs from those of other advanced nations, and on the nature and importance of the contribution of structure to economic performance.

The Department of Applied Economics at Cambridge has gone a long way in recent years towards rectifying the absence of information on economies of scale through the combined work of Pratten, Dean and Silberston,[3] but this has been done mainly in a British context. This work has emphasised that in many industries economies of scale continue up to levels of output which are substantial in relation to the overall size of British markets, and that technological developments are causing these economies to become even more significant. Generally the economies come primarily from technical sources, augmented by savings in marketing, research and development and management.

With regard to differences between countries in the structure of industries, the major pioneering work has been carried out by J.S. Bain.[4] He compared the average size of the largest twenty plants and firms (as measured by employment) in up to 34 industries in eight countries.[5] His findings for plants were that overall the largest units were in the United States with the UK having plants on average about three-quarters this size. Sizes in the other nations were substantially lower, ranging from 13 to 39 per cent of the US level. The results for firms showed broadly the same relative distribution, but with smaller differentials, due to the tendency for firms in non-US industries to operate more plants.

Although providing a substantial increase in our knowledge of international variations in industrial structure, Bain's work tends to give a misleading impression.

1 H. Leibenstein, 'Allocative Efficiency versus X-Efficiency', *American Economic Review*, June 1966, pp. 392–415.

2 R.M. Cyert and K.D. George, 'Competition, Growth and Efficiency', *Economic Journal*, March 1969, pp. 23–41.

3 C. Pratten and R.M. Dean, (in collaboration with A. Silberston), *The Economies of Large-Scale Production in British Industry*, University of Cambridge, Department of Applied Economics, Occasional Paper 3, (Cambridge: Cambridge University Press), 1965; C. Pratten *Economies of Scale in Manufacturing Industry*, University of Cambridge, Department of Applied Economics, Occasional Paper 28, (Cambridge: Cambridge University Press), 1971, and A. Silberston, 'Economies of Scale in Theory and Practice', *Economic Journal*, Supplement, March 1972, pp. 369–390.

4 J.S. Bain, *International Differences in Industrial Structure*, (New York: Yale University Press), 1966.

5 The countries of his sample were: Canada, France, India, Italy, Japan, Sweden, U.S.A., UK.

It underestimates size differences through using employment as an indicator, since at the time of the investigation labour productivity was substantially higher in the USA than elsewhere. Thus production units in the US with outputs equal to and identical with those of units elsewhere appear smaller on the basis of an employment comparison. In addition, a distortion is introduced through basing the comparison upon the average size of an absolute and constant number of units in each country (the largest twenty). The smaller is a country's industry, the more is its average depressed by the inclusion of progessively smaller and less important units which may operate under markedly different technical, cost or demand conditions from the units producing the bulk of output. Bain's work is further limited because it did not study any individual industry in depth, neither did it give any indication of inter-country differences in product-mix, the range of products in relation to the markets or vertical integration.

In 1966 G.F. Ray compared large plants (employing more than 1,000 people) in the UK and West Germany and found that in Germany these were on average larger in terms of employment than in the UK and had substantially higher labour productivity. These relationships were particularly marked in the export industries.[1] But again, no detailed industry analysis was carried out.

Phlips has examined cross-country differences in concentration between four of the founder members of the EEC (Belgium, France, Italy and the Netherlands) and has studied the relationships between concentration levels and selected performance indicators.[2] A direct comparison of employment concentration ratios for the four largest enterprises in up to 93 industry groups shows the median concentration values to be highest for Luxembourg, followed by Belgium and the Netherlands (each with broadly comparable levels), France and Italy. However, these results are substantially qualified by the influence on concentration levels of cross-country differences in the sizes of markets and of firms. With equal-sized firms, increases in market size will reduce concentration ratios, while larger firm size, given a constant market, will raise concentration levels. A regression analysis by Phlips taking account of these factors (by considering total industry employment and average firm employment size) shows France to have systematically the highest level of concentration. As market size increases concentration decreases at the fastest rate in the Netherlands, and Belgium and Italy have comparable and low concentration levels. Phlips suggests that the high concentration levels in France are attributable to the protected nature of industry together with the prevalence of *de facto* cartels. In the analysis of the concentration-performance links, Phlips finds that high profit levels are positively connected with high concentration and high entry barriers, that wage rates are positively related to concentration, and that on the basis of data for Belgium only, the intensity of research activity generally increases with the level of concentration. No connection is found, however, between concentration ratios and price inflation.

1   G.F. Ray, 'The Size of Plants: A Comparison', N.I.E.S.R. *Review*, November, 1966, pp. 63–6.

2   L. Phlips, *Effects of Industrial Concentration*, (Amsterdam: North Holland), 1971.

Recently more attention has been paid to the relationships between cross-country differences in industrial structure and trade performance by Nicholas Owen.[1] The first part of his enquiry has concerned the isolation of the principal determinants of bilateral trade advantage between the three larger founder members of the EEC, France, West Germany and Italy. Bilateral trade advantage is defined as the ratio of the dollar value of the difference in trade between each pair of countries in a given commodity to the dollar value of their combined trade with each other in that commodity. Use of this ratio removes the influence of inter-industry differences in the absolute value of the trade advantage, which varies with the economic importance of the commodity. The trade data refer to 1964, the earliest date for which the formation of the EEC could be expected to influence trade integration. A multi-variate regression analysis was employed, which showed the prime determinants of trade advantage variations to be differences in the relative sizes of firms and plants (measured by the ratio of the employment sizes of the twenty largest units in 1962), with plant size being the stronger influence by a considerable margin. Differences in the relative overall scale of industry, in capital intensiveness and in labour productivity are found to be insignificant.

The second part of the study indicates the influence on total bilateral trade by industries of the degree of concentration in the national market at the level of the eight largest firms. The overall level of output in each pair of countries exercises the greatest effect upon their combined level of inter-trade. However, market concentration is found to contribute a substantial and positive effect up to a threshold employment concentration level of between 45 and 60 per cent (i.e. inter-trade increases with concentration from low values of the latter). At the threshold an important shift in the function occurs, with inter-trade levels falling substantially and regaining their former maximum level only at concentration rates approaching 100 per cent. The important implication of this is that in atomistic industries, rises in concentration and increases in firm size aid trade performance, but that at the threshold oligopolistic interdependence on a cross-national basis substantially impedes trade.

These studies are of great value but there is a continuing need for further research into cross-country differences in industrial structure and the relations with performance variations — matters of great importance for businessmen, academic economists and Goverment policy makers at both national and supra-national levels alike. Specifically, until the present, no studies have been based upon a detailed comparison of individual industries. We have endeavoured to rectify this in our work, the first fruits of which are contained in this volume on the steel industry.

Our work has been directed to the following groups of questions:

(a) To what extent do industry structures differ between countries?
In discussing structure we are interested not only in international variations in overall plant and firm sizes but also in such aspects as differences in techniques employed, product-mixes, production runs and vertical integration. Since most previous work has taken data from official censuses of production which are to differing degrees out of date, and which are highly aggregated and measure size in employment terms,

---

1 Nicholas Owen, *Intra-EEC Trade and Industry Structure*, (London: Department of Trade and Industry), mimeo, 1973; summarised in Nicholas Owen, 'Competition and industrial structure: implications of entry to the EEC', *Trade and Industry*, 22 March 1973, pp. 586–88.

we have tried very hard to develop recent measures using units of physical output or capacity.

(b) What are the chief sources of economies of scale and over what scale ranges do they operate? Does the extent of scale economies differ between countries as a result of variations in market conditions, technology, or factor prices? Has the extent of economies of scale changed recently?

(c) How far are the scale economies which are available in each country actually achieved? Have changes in industrial structure been able to keep pace with technological developments?

(d) What connection is there between the differences in the scales of industries and the differences in their performances? What are the other principal factors which appear to affect performance?

(e) Can changes be made in structures to allow some improvement in performance? If so, how might these best be attempted?

The countries we have selected for our enquiry are the United Kingdom (UK), United States of America (US), Canada, Japan, and the founder members of the European Economic Community (EEC) — Belgium-Luxembourg, France, the Federal Republic of Germany (Germany, FR), Italy and the Netherlands.[1]

The present enquiry is concerned with the production of semi-finished and finished steel goods. Steel may be defined as an alloy of pure iron with less than two per cent carbon by weight.[2] In general, the range of activities considered are those included in group 341 (Iron and Steel Basic Industries) of the revised International Standard Industrial Classification.[3] These are iron smelting; crude steel manufacture, the production of billets, blooms slabs or bars, re-rolling and drawing into basic forms such as sheet, plates, strip, tubes, pipes, rails, rods and wire, and the production of tin-plate rough castings and forgings.[4]

The arrangement of the study of the steel industry in this paper is as follows. The two initial sections set the background for the subsequent analysis by examining recent trends in output, demand and foreign trade (Section II), and the trends in investment together with the development of technology (Section III). Section IV indicates the structure of costs and prices. Section V compares plant and firm sizes. In the next section (VI) the recent development of the industry is described in each country in turn. Section VII reviews the available evidence on economies of scale, and Section VIII relates these findings to the observed inter-country variations in

---

1 Belgium and Luxembourg are united in an economic union, therefore we treat them as a single country. In the context of the present steel industry enquiry, the EEC members formed the European Coal and Steel Community (ECSC) in 1952 under the Treaty of Paris, six years prior to the establishment of the wider European Economic Community. The two communities were merged in 1968, and for convenience we use the EEC appelation throughout.

2 H.E. McGannon (ed), *The Making, Shaping and Treating of Steel*, (New York: United States Steel Corporation),8th edition, 1964. The processes involved in the manufacture of the main classes of steel product are briefly described in Appendix 1 to this paper.

3 Statistical Office of the United Nations, *Indexes to the International Standard Industrial Classification of all Economic Activities*, Statistical Papers, series M, No. 4, Rev. 1 Add. 1, (New York: United Nations), 1965.

4 See Appendix 1 for definitions of the less obvious of these terms.

6

structure. The last part of the analysis (Section IX) is a study of the relationship between the degree of attainment of scale economies and export performance. Section X summarises the conclusions of the study and considers their implications.

Throughout the study cost and price data are given in US$, converted at exchange rates prevailing at the date to which the data relate. Unless specifically stated otherwise, all output quantities are given in metric tons (= 0.9842 gross tons), and refer to annual rates. Because of rounding the detail of tables may not sum to totals.

II

Output, Demand and Foreign Trade

The nine countries of this enquiry differ substantially in terms of their overall level of crude steel output. The largest producer is the United States with annual output rates approaching 130 million tons, twenty-six times the output of the smallest producer, the Netherlands. Column 2 of Table 1 sets out the level of crude steel production in each country in 1969.[1] The table also gives the average annual increase in production between 1950 and 1969 in both quantity and percentage terms. The highest rates of expansion of production have been in Japan, the Netherlands and Italy, with the US having the slowest expansion rate. As steel is an important capital goods industry in all countries, these growth rates are usually closely connected with trend changes in total real national income. Of considerable importance to our later consideration of achievements of economies of scale are the average incremental annual *quantity* increases in production which occurred during the period and which are shown in column 3. Because of absolute differences in the sizes of the industries these are not at all closely linked with the growth rates; the greatest annual quantity increases occur in Japan, which has the highest *rate* of growth, and in the US, which has the lowest.

Superimposed on the trend movements in steel production are cyclical variations resulting in part from an acceleration effect, through which changes in expenditure on consumption goods have a magnified effect upon capital goods expenditure. The cyclical fluctuations for the countries of the enquiry during the period 1950–1968 are examined in detail in Appendix 2. Each set of data exhibits cyclical movements over at least part of the period. Boom years, in which output increased at a faster rate than in the immediately preceeding or succeeding periods are easily identified. General booms occurred in 1955/6, 1959/60 and, particularly, in 1964, indicating a four-to-five year cycle in most areas, a tendency which is marked in the period after 1959. In Japan, which has enjoyed consistently high rates of growth, the cyclical tendency is marked by variations in the annual percentage rates of increase, rather than by absolute increases and decreases in production.

---

1 Crude steel production is the most convenient indicator of the level of physical output. Finished steel output is slightly less than that for crude steel (because of losses during rolling and processing) and differs as a proportion of crude steel output between the countries (because of product-mix variations) but gives broadly comparable orders of magnitude. Pig-iron production is usually about one-half of crude steel output, the proportion varying depending upon the combination of raw materials used for steel-making and the importance of imports.

Table 1   *Crude Steel Production 1969 and Average Annual Increases, 1950–1969, by Country*

Country	Production 1969	Average Annual Increase 1950–1969	
	m. tons	m. tons	%[a]
Belgium-Luxembourg	18.4	0.6	5.0
France	22.5	0.6	3.0
Germany, F.R.	45.3	1.7	6.8
Italy	16.4	0.7	13.3
Netherlands	4.7	0.2	21.6
E.E.C.	107.3	4.0	6.4
U.K.	26.8	0.5	2.7
U.S.	128.2	2.1	1.8
Canada	9.4	0.3	8.2
Japan	82.2	4.1	34.0[b]

Notes:
(a) Compound trend annual rates of increase, calculated from least-squares regression line for each time-series.
(b) 1952–1969.
Source: British Steel Corporation, *Statistical Handbook*, 1969, (London) 1970.

In the context of the UK industry, Blake[1] has noted that steel output fluctuates considerably more than the consumption of domestically-produced steel. This relationship is also apparent from our data for every other country in the enquiry. Blake attributes the over-response of production to changes in demand to the inevitably slow adjustment of production to a shift in demand. When an increase in steel consumption is anticipated, customers and stockholders over-order to ensure their supplies. If manufacturers plan to produce to meet all their orders, many of which are subsequently cancelled, stocks build up, resulting in a severe reduction in demand for steel producers.[2] To alleviate this he suggests closer cooperation and communication between the producers and their final customers; for the UK this could be achieved in part by more forward integration into stockholding on the part of the producers, a proposal we examine again later.

In Table 2, the composition of the final output of steel products in each country is analysed. Two broad categories of product are distinguished: *flat-rolled products*, comprising plate, sheet and strip and *light and heavy rolled*, including rods, bars, sections, semis for tubes, and railway track material. Flat-rolled products form the bulk of total output in each country, their share being particularly high in the Netherlands, the USA and Canada. In the case of the two last countries, this reflects the importance of the consumer durable goods industries (and automobiles in particular) in the economy. Of light and heavy rolled products, bars, rods (excluding wire) and light sections form the majority of output in each country. With the exception of Japan, where strip and coil accounts for forty per cent of total output, there is no evidence of marked product specialisation between the countries of the table.

1 Christopher Blake, 'Supply Lags and Demand Acceleration in the United Kingdom Steel Industry', *Scottish Journal of Political Economy*, Vol. 12 1965, pp. 62–80.

2 Customers' stocks also fluctuate a good deal, for similar reasons.

Table 2   *Percentage Composition of Output of Finished Steel Products, by Class of Product and Country, 1969 (US 1968)*

Class of Product	Belgium-Luxembourg %	France %	Germany %	Italy %	Netherlands %	E.E.C. %	U.K. %	U.S.(a) %	Canada %	Japan %
Plates : heavy	0.3	0.6	1.8	0.2	16.1	1.6	18.0	10.8		17.9
light & medium	14.4	11.8	16.6	12.6	0.8	13.9				1.4
Sheet	27.7	14.0	21.7	22.9	0.5	20.1	30.7	14.7	61.8	40.0
Strip and coil	12.5	25.2	15.9	15.5	61.5	19.4	9.7	10.8		
Flat-Rolled Products	54.9	51.6	56.0	51.1	78.9	54.9	58.4	63.3	61.8	59.3
Wire Rods	8.9	12.7	10.6	6.5	8.3	10.1	10.3	5.3	5.8	5.6
Other bars, rods, light sections	26.6	23.0	19.8	34.9	12.0	23.7	16.1	15.9	21.2	12.1
Heavy Sections	8.2	7.8	7.6	4.0	–	6.8	11.5	5.9	5.8	–
Rounds and Squares for Tubes	0.7	3.1	4.6	2.5	0.8	3.2	2.3	4.4	1.6	2.1
Railway Track Material	0.5	1.8	1.4	1.0	–	1.3	1.4	0.9	3.7	0.8
Light and heavy rolled products	44.9	48.4	44.0	48.9	22.1	45.0	41.6	32.4	38.1	20.6
Other not elsewhere classified	0.2	–	–	–	–	–	–	4.3	–	20.1
Total	100.0	100.0	100.0	100.0	100.0	100.0	100.0	100.0	100.0	100.0
Total Production (million tons)	9.8	17.3	31.9	12.9	3.0	75.0	20.2	87.9	7.1	66.9

Notes: (a) 1968.
Source: As for Table 1.

Table 3   *Apparent Consumption of Steel (in Crude Steel Equivalent) 1969 and Average Annual Increase, 1950–1969, by Country*

Country	Apparent Consumption 1969 m. tons	Average Annual Increase 1950–1969 %[a]
Belgium-Luxembourg	4.5	4.5
France	22.5	5.4
Germany, F.R.	37.4	6.1
Italy	19.0	12.9
Netherlands	5.1	5.3
E.E.C.	88.5	7.1
U.K.	24.1	2.5
U.S.	137.8	2.7
Canada	10.5	5.6
Japan	61.8	22.6[b]

Notes:
(a) Compound trend annual rate of increase.
(b) 1952–1969.
   Source: As for Table 1.

The levels and recent trends in demand in the countries of the enquiry are given in Table 3. Demand is represented by the apparent consumption of crude steel, defined as production *minus* exports *plus* imports. A comparison with Table 1 shows that the consumption of crude steel is of broadly the same order of magnitude in each country as its production; the most notable exception is Belgium-Luxembourg, where the importance of exports carries production to a level four times higher than consumption. The same relationship is apparent when the trends in the growth of production and consumption are compared: high rates of production expansion are generally associated with high rates of increase in consumption.

In 1969, the production of crude steel exceeded its consumption — indicating a trade surplus on a volume basis — in four of the countries *viz*., Belgium-Luxembourg, Germany F.R., the UK and Japan. Trade deficits occurred in Italy, the Netherlands, the US and Canada, with France obtaining a balance. In the surplus countries the trend has been for the rate of increase of production to exceed that of consumption, indicating a strengthening trade balance. Of the deficit countries the tendency has been for the export shortfall to reduce in three (Italy, the Netherlands and Canada) and to increase in the US. The trade position of France has tended to deteriorate.

Table 4 expands this by analysing the trends in the share of exports in production and of imports in apparent consumption between 1950 and 1969. The first part of the table shows that exports form an important part of total production in each country with the exception of the US. Their importance is greatest in Belgium-Luxembourg and the Netherlands. Again with the exception of the US the general trend since 1960 has been for exports to increase their share of total production. The second part of the table analyses imports. Here their share of apparent consumption has tended to increase during the period in all countries except Japan. The almost complete absence of imports in that country results both from restrictions on the volume of imports permitted and, since the late 1960s at least, from the low prices charged by domestic producers which have made exporting by other

11

Table 4   *Percentage of (a) Total Production formed by Exports, (b) Apparent Consumption formed by Imports (Crude Steel Equivalents), 1950–1969, by Country*

(a) *Exports as a Percentage of Total Production*

Country	1950–59	1960–64	Period 1965 Percentages	1966	1967	1968	1969
Belgium-Luxembourg	77.9	84.0	89.5	88.6	88.4	88.6	90.1
France	36.0	40.3	44.1	42.2	43.2	44.4	39.9
Germany F.R.	22.1	31.5	34.2	35.7	42.6	40.6	45.7
Italy	11.7	15.4	26.1	21.2	18.0	19.5	15.9
Netherlands	58.1	78.2	87.8	85.7	93.6	91.9	91.0
E.E.C.	35.9	41.1	46.1	45.0	47.5	47.7	49.5
U.K.	17.0	16.2	17.9	18.5	20.7	21.1	18.7
U.S.	4.7	3.4	2.6	1.8	1.9	2.3	5.0
Canada	8.4	16.7	13.3	13.9	15.0	19.8	14.7
Japan	16.1	16.5	29.9	25.8	18.5	25.2	25.0

(b) *Imports as a Percentage of Apparent Consumption*

Country	1950–59	1960–64	Period 1965 Percentages	1966	1967	1968	1969
Belgium-Luxembourg	14.9	37.3	52.1	56.5	58.0	53.7	59.7
France	8.2	29.7	31.7	33.8	37.5	37.1	39.8
Germany F.R.	13.6	19.6	23.3	25.0	24.9	30.1	35.0
Italy	17.0	31.8	21.4	24.2	23.3	21.1	27.4
Netherlands	82.5	85.9	89.4	88.4	94.8	93.1	91.6
E.E.C.	17.0	28.8	29.9	32.3	33.6	34.4	39.1
U.K.	6.0	6.5	3.3	5.3	10.1	12.1	11.1
U.S.	1.9	4.8	9.2	9.3	10.5	15.3	11.7
Canada	31.7	18.4	24.1	18.9	19.1	16.8	24.4
Japan	2.1	0.9	0.1	0.1	1.0	0.3	0.3

Source: as for Table 1.

nations unprofitable. The most substantial increase in the penetration of imports has occurred in the US, where their share rose from an average of less than two per cent in 1950–1959 to over 15 per cent in 1968. The previous part of the table shows that there has been no commensurate increase in exports, and this trend has caused great concern to the US industry recently.[1] A notable feature of the whole table is the rising trend of trade in all the EEC countries: this reflects in particular the growing importance of trade between the members.

1   See particularly Committee on Finance, US Senate, *Steel Imports*, (Washington, D.C.: US. Government Printing Office), 1967 and American Iron and Steel Institute, *Steel Imports – A National Concern*, (Washington, D.C.) 1970.

III

Investment and Technology

Table 5 details the recent trends in total investment expenditure and in investment per ton of annual output in the iron and steel industries of the countries of the enquiry. As the figures for 1969 show, there is a wide range of variation between the countries, both in terms of their total investment expenditure and in terms of their investment per output ton. Broadly, the larger the output of the industry, the greater is the total investment expenditure : the ranking of the countries by their 1969 total investment closely parallels the ranking by total crude steel production in that year (see Table 1). The major exception is the UK which ranks fourth in terms of production, but eighth in terms of investment. However, the connection between output and total investment expenditure is not directly proportional; so that investment per unit of output does not closely relate to the level of production — between 1966 and 1969 the Netherlands with the smallest level of production obtained the highest rate of investment per unit of output. By contrast, the UK, after the investment boom of 1961/62 secured the lowest investment rate.

The trend in investment expenditure during the period covered by the table in the EEC countries was variously downward (for Belgium-Luxembourg, France and Germany, F.R.), upward (for the Netherlands), and erratic (for Italy). However, each country also exhibits cyclical fluctuations with peaks generally occurring in the boom production periods (1963/4 and 1968/9). Of the other countries the trend of investment was downwards in the UK, upwards in both the US and Japan and fairly constant in Canada, which was the only one of these nations to produce distinctly cyclical variations. Public sector provision of investment funds has been important in France (under the Vth and VIth National Plans), in Italy, and, especially since nationalisation in 1967, in the UK.

OECD data on the application of investment in the steel industries of the EEC countries and the UK indicate that in 1969 roughly one-half (47 per cent) of the total expenditure was used in the provision of facilities at the finishing stage — hot and cold rolling mills, heat treatment plant, etc. The next largest category of expenditure, accounting for 20 per cent of the total, was at the crude steel stage, followed by expenditure for raw materials (10 per cent), ancillary plant (15 per cent), and pig iron (8 per cent). These relative shares had been broadly maintained throughout the 1960s.[1]

---

1 Special Committee for Iron and Steel, *The Iron and Steel Industry in 1969*, (Paris: OECD), 1970, Table 37.

Table 5 *Investment and Investment per Output ton, Iron and Steel Industry, 1962–1969: by Country*

Country	1962		1963		1964		1965		1966		1967		1968		1969	
	$m	$/t	$m	$/t	$m	$/t	$m	$/t	$m	$/t	$m	$/t	$m	$/t	$m	$/t
Belgium-Luxembourg	179	15.8	197	17.0	163	12.3	167	21.1	171	22.5	116	14.5	88	9.2	116	16.5
France	437	25.3	325	18.5	207	10.5	165	8.6	148	7.5	170	9.1	253	12.4	273	12.1
Germany, F.R.	414	12.7	443	14.0	379	10.2	312	8.5	294	8.3	224	6.1	225	5.5	310	6.8
Italy	159	16.8	448	44.1	519	53.0	246	19.4	167	12.2	126	8.0	111	6.6	143	8.7
Netherlands	53	25.4	56	23.9	48	18.1	37	11.8	68	21.0	95	27.8	125	33.7	124	26.4
E.E.C.	1242	17.1	1496	20.1	1316	15.9	932	10.8	848	10.0	730	8.3	802	8.1	1017	9.5
U.K. (a)	476	22.9	215	9.4	154	5.8	139	5.1	117	4.7	136	5.6	119	4.5	102	3.8
U.S.	904	10.0	1040	10.5	1600	13.9	1823	15.2	1953	16.1	2173	18.8	2372	19.9	2136	16.7
Canada	101	15.5	99	13.4	191	23.1	151	16.6	195	21.5	114	13.0	61	5.9	95	10.1
Japan	618	22.4	461	14.6	460	11.6	454	11.0	540	11.3	842	13.6	1167	17.4	1494	18.2

Notes: (a) From 1967, investment expenditure of BSC only.
Sources: Special Committee for Iron and Steel, *The Iron and Steel Industry in 1964*; (Paris: OECD), 1965, Table 39; ditto, *in 1970*: (Paris: OECD), 1971; BSC data.

Table 6   *Number and Average Size of Blast Furnaces by Country, 1960, 1968 (Canada 1967)*

Country	1960 Furnaces in blast number	1960 Average Size m. tons	1968 Furnaces in blast number	1968 Average Size m. tons
Belgium-Luxembourg	81	$0.3^{(a)}$	67	$0.4^{(a)}$
France	120	$0.1^{(a)}$	74	$0.2^{(a)}$
Germany F.R.	n.a.	n.a.	n.a.	n.a.
Italy	n.a.	n.a.	n.a.	n.a.
Netherlands	n.a.	n.a.	n.a.	n.a.
E.E.C.	n.a.	n.a.	n.a.	n.a.
U.K.	85	$0.2^{(a)}$	54	$0.3^{(a)}$
U.S.	229	$0.4^{(b)}$	154	$0.5^{(a)}$
Canada	16	$0.3^{(b)}$	14	$0.5^{(b)}$
Japan	34	$0.3^{(b)}$	n.a.	$0.8^{(b)}$

Notes: (a) Output
(b) Capacity
Source: BISF/BSC, *Statistical Handbooks, 1961–8*, (London), 1961–8; Japan Iron and Steel
Federation, *The Steel Industry of Japan 1969*, (Tokyo) 1969.

Commenting on the nature of recent investment projects in the OECD countries
(which include Austria, Spain and Sweden as well as those in this enquiry) the
Special Committee for Iron and Steel define three major trends.[1] The first is the
modernisation of existing plant and equipment, the second the rationalisation of
production and distribution, both within and between firms, frequently following
mergers, and thirdly, and most importantly, the construction of new works or the
substantial expansion of existing ones.

In recent years there have been extensive technological developments at all stages
of the iron and steel making process. In pig iron production the improved burdens
now available, higher blowing rates and blast temperatures, the use of high top
pressure, and size increases upto 400 cu.m. have enabled modern blast furnaces to
produce up to 10,000 tons of pig iron a day (or nearly 3.5 million tons annually)
using a high-grade haematite ore. As Table 6 shows, for the countries for which
information is available, the trend in recent years has been for the numbers of
furnaces in blast to decline, and for their average capacities to increase. In addition
to the increasing scale of pig iron production, current research in most countries is
directed towards the direct reduction of iron ore to steel, by-passing entirely the
blast-furnace stage. To date this technique has been applied commercially in mini-
works in Hamburg (Germany, F.R.) and Georgetown (US) as well as elsewhere.

Table 7 shows the trends in the proportions of total crude steel output contributed
by the major techniques of production in the five main areas covered by this enquiry.
Comparable data for the individual members of the EEC are given in Table 8. The
rise in the importance of the basic oxygen system (BOS) since 1954 is readily
apparent. The most marked development of the BOS was in Japan, where by 1968
it accounted for almost three-quarters of the total output of crude steel. The technique also became important in each of the member countries of the EEC, (Table 8)
although for reasons considered in more detail below, its development in France

1   Ibid., p. 67.

15

Table 7 *Percentage Composition of Crude Steel Output by Type of Process and Area, 1950, 1960, 1968 (Canada 1967)*

	Percentage Composition of Crude Steel Output														
	E.E.C.			U.K.			U.S.			Canada(b)			Japan		
	1954	1964	1968	1954	1964	1968	1954	1964	1968	1954	1964	1967	1954	1964	1968
Basic Oxygen System	–	12.7	32.7	–	10.5	23.9	–	12.2	37.1	–	28.4	40.0	–	44.2	73.7
Electric Arc	8.6	10.9	13.1	5.0	11.2	16.1	6.2	10.0	12.8	15.8	11.8	13.8	13.2	21.0	18.2
Open Hearth	40.7	34.0	25.9	87.7	70.5	54.8	91.0	77.2	50.1	84.2	60.3	52.2	82.1	34.8	8.1
Other	50.7	42.4	28.3	7.3	7.8	5.2	2.9	0.7	(a)	–	–	–	4.7	–	–
Total	100.0	100.0	100.0	100.0	100.0	100.0	100.0	100.0	100.0	100.0	100.0	100.0	100.0	100.0	100.0
Production (m. tons)	41.0	81.9	98.6	18.8	26.7	26.3	80.1	115.2	119.3	4.2	8.2	10.6	7.7	39.8	66.9

Notes: –: nil
   (a) included with open hearth
   (b) capacity data

Source: All areas except Canada, BISF/BSC *Statistical Handbooks 1960–8*; Canada: J. Singer, *Trade Liberalisation and the Canadian Steel Industry*, (Toronto: University of Toronto Press) 1969, Table 1 p. 4.

Table 8 Percentage Composition of Crude Steel Output by Type of Process and Area, EEC Countries, 1954, 1964, 1968

Type of Process	Belgium-Luxembourg			France			Germany			Italy			Netherlands		
	1954	1964	1968	1954	1964	1968	1954	1964	1968	1954	1964	1968	1954	1964	1968
Basic Oxygen System	–	6.8	37.0	–	11.4	18.2	–	14.2	37.1	–	2.4	28.7	–	69.5	62.6
Electric Arc	2.8	3.6	2.7	7.8	7.7	10.1	3.9	6.8	9.0	40.0	43.2	37.9	13.3	8.2	7.6
Open Hearth	6.4	3.4	1.2	32.0	26.5	20.0	56.2	45.6	35.3	52.5	49.9	33.4	86.7	22.2	29.7
Other	90.9	86.2	59.1	60.2	54.4	51.8	39.9	33.3	18.6	7.5	4.6	–/–	–	–	–
Total	100.0	100.0	100.0	100.0	100.0	100.0	100.0	100.0	100.0	100.0	100.0	100.0	100.0	100.0	100.0
Production (m. tons)	7.8	13.3	16.4	10.6	19.5	20.4	17.4	36.7	41.2	4.2	9.8	17.0	0.9	2.6	3.7

Notes: – nil
          –/– less than 0.1 per cent
Source: as for Table 7.

17

was comparatively slow. The BOS was developed and first commercially applied in Austria in the early 1950s[1]. For the countries included in this enquiry the first such facility was installed in 1954 in the US[2]. As the analysis of cost conditions in Section IV below indicates the process generally has the advantages of lower raw material, conversion and capital charges per ton of crude steel produced as compared with other available techniques; however, it must be incorporated in an integrated plant with blast furnaces, since it requires at least 70 per cent of its charge to be of hot metal. In the UK, US, Canada and Japan, the rise in importance of the BOS has been almost entirely at the expense of the open hearth technique, which now is regarded as obsolete. In the EEC, BOS production developed at the expense of both open hearth and "other" techniques, which are almost entirely basic bessemer (Thomas) converters. In Belgium-Luxembourg (Table 8) the reduction in the relative importance of the Thomas process accounted for almost the whole of the increased share of total output contributed by the BOS.

Over the period of the analysis, the relative importance of the electric arc furnace increased in all countries except Canada, the Netherlands and Italy (where nonetheless it accounted for the majority of crude steel output in 1968). The increased share held by these furnaces probably reflects to a small extent the expansion of special steel production, for which they are essential. However, the major factors have been the overall expansion of economic activity in most of the countries which has increased the supply of scrap, and the replacement of the open-hearth process by the BOS technique, which has reduced the proportion of scrap which the large-scale steel works can absorb.

Despite the development of the BOS, Thomas converters are still very important in Belgium-Luxembourg and France, where they accounted for over one-half of total crude steel production in 1968. The technique has retained its dominance both because of the availability of high-phosphorous iron ore (for the reduction of which it is particularly suited) from Lorraine, and more recently because of the development of a technique in which pure oxygen is blown into the bottom of the converter. This increases the output rate and allows a wider range of ores to be used. The importance of the Thomas process is expected to decline sharply in the near future in both countries. This is because a recently developed process, Oxygen-Lance-Poudre (OLP), permits the BOS to accept high-phosphorous ores. The Chambre Syndicale de la Sidérurgie Française estimates that the Thomas process will have disappeared completely by 1980.

There can be no doubt that the BOS will increase in importance in all the countries of the enquiry during this next decade. The BOS installations of the countries included in this enquiry are analysed in Table 9. Germany, F.R. has the largest installations on average, but the largest single installation, with an annual capacity of 7.6 million tons, is in Japan.

Traditionally crude steel is tapped from the furnace and cast into large ingot moulds. The hot ingots are then rolled into blooms, billets and slabs. Efforts are

1 By Voest and Oesterreichisch-Alpine Montangesellschaft at their plants at Linz and Donawitz respectively; hence the description L-D for one type of B.O.S.

2 By the McLouth Steel Corp., at their plant in Trenton, Mich. (see Staff Study of the Committee on Finance, op. cit, 1967).

18

Table 9   *Basic Oxygen Installations: Numbers of Installations and Furnaces, Total Capacity, Average Size of Installations and Size of Largest Installation, by Country, 1970 (estimated)*

Country	Installations Number	Furnaces Number	Total Annual Capacity Million tons	Average Annual Capacity of Installations '000 tons	Annual Capacity of largest Installations '000 tons
Belgium-Luxembourg	12	21	11.4	952.2	2204.5
France	9	14	6.6	731.0	3810.2
Germany, F.R.	13	35	35.2	2710.4	5987.5
Italy	4	11	10.7	2676.2	5806.1
Netherlands	2	5	4.8	2376.9	2503.9
E.E.C.	40	86	68.7	1717.5	5987.5
U.K.	8	20	13.9	1732.8	3311.3
U.S.	34	76	71.0	2087.9	4263.8
Canada	3	7	4.0	1336.6	2540.2
Japan	36	89	96.1	2670.4	6894.7
Total	121	278	253.7	2096.6	6894.7

Source: Kaiser Engineers, *L-D Process Newsletter*, (Chicago) October 1971.

currently being made to develop and perfect systems of continuous casting, in which the molten steel is poured into a long tube of the required cross-section and continuously withdrawn from the other end as it solidifies. The benefits of this are that the intermediate stages of ingot casting and primary rolling are removed, but it is necessary to be able to produce long runs of a product of constant quality and cross-sectional dimensions, and to have a steady flow of hot metal from the furnace. This last factor affects the organisation of the earlier steel-making stage since it requires a number of furnaces to be in operation, and thus for all except the largest plants, reduces the maximum size of individual furnaces which it is possible to use. The introduction of the technique has been inhibited by technical problems affecting the quality of the steel cast, and by the difficulty of obtaining sufficiently long runs. The OECD provides an indication of the importance of continuously cast steel relative to that produced by the traditional method for all the countries of this enquiry with the exception of the US and Japan, for which data are not available.[1] In 1969, continuously cast steel as a proportion of total production was highest in Canada (11.8 per cent), followed by Germany, F.R. (7.3 per cent), Italy (3.1 per cent), UK (1.8 per cent) and France (0.6 per cent). Belgium-Luxembourg and the Netherlands produced no steel by this method.

At the finishing stage, the maximum capacities of rolling mills have been expanded considerably in recent years through increases in the power of the driving motors, increases in rolling speeds, reductions in change-over times for rolling a product of different dimensions, and the development of automatic gauge control. Primary mills with annual capacities of up to 10 million tons are available, while the maximum size of a hot strip mill is about 5 million tons and that for a bar mill is probably around 0.5 million tons.[2] Developments have also enabled the rate of throughput to be raised significantly in heat treatment, galvanising and tinning operations. The introduction of electric resistance welding in tube manufacture has also substantially raised efficiency.

1   Special Committee for Iron and Steel, op. cit., 1970, Table 4.

2   These orders of magnitude were suggested during discussions with steel industry respondents in the U.S.

IV

The Structure of Costs and Prices

In this section, we illustrate first the importance of the various cost components in steel-making and then consider the effect of technology upon costs. Finally we examine the extent of international variations in costs resulting from differences in factor prices.

Table 10 *Dispersion of Revenue per ton of Crude Steel Produced in Integrated Steelworks, British Steel Corporation, Financial Year 1970–71*

Item	Dispersion of Revenue	
	$ per ton	Percentage
Consumption of:		
Ore	12.02	9.36
Purchased Scrap	10.06	7.84
Other raw materials	18.39	14.32
Coal, coke, fuel and power	14.84	11.56
Stores, spares and other maintenance materials (inc. contractors charges)	12.32	9.60
Operating supplies	6.69	5.21
Materials bought-in	74.32	57.89
Salaries, wages and associated costs	32.54	25.34
Carriage outwards and delivery charges	4.63	3.61
Other costs (net of sundry credits)	6.50	5.06
Cost of Sales	117.99	91.89
Net depreciation, interest, loss provision and taxation	7.62	5.94
Revenue surplus after tax	2.79	2.18
Total	128.41	100.00
Total revenue ($m)	3,222.37	
Crude steel output (m. tons)	25.10	

Source: British Steel Corporation, *Annual Report and Accounts,* 1970–71, (London) 1971, pp. 86 and 88.

(a) Orders of Magnitude

Table 10 shows the dispersion of revenue per ton of crude steel produced in integrated steelworks by the British Steel Corporation in 1970–71. The unit values, which for comparative purposes are given in US$, tend to over-estimate the importance of each component of revenue, since the total revenue data from which they are derived relate to the receipts from the sale of all iron and steel products, and include, *inter alia*, the costs of finishing processes after the steelmaking stage. However, the table gives a broad indication of the relevant magnitudes.

Purchases of materials and supplies comprise well over one-half of total revenue receipts, and labour expenses form about one-quarter. When related to value added (revenue minus purchases), however, labour costs become much more important, accounting for 60 per cent of the total.

(b) Costs and Technology

Currently there are two best-practice routes for the production of steel products. The blast furnace — basic oxygen converter route is best suited for the large-scale production of steel for rolling into a wide range of finished forms, particularly sheet and strip. The electric arc furnace route, making crude steel from scrap, is suited to the small-scale production both of high-quality special steels and of common grades for rolling as bars and rods. The previous section showed that these two routes are accounting for increasing proportions of crude steel production.

A general idea of the production costs associated with these two processes (and for comparison those of the obsolete open-hearth process), based on UK data, are presented in Tables 11 and 12. The first table gives estimates of the raw material input requirements and costs per ton of crude steel output. Two sets of estimates are given for the open-hearth process, according to whether a cold or hot metal charge is used, in order to indicate the wide range of unit costs which can result. The table shows that in each system slightly more than one ton of material is required for each ton of crude steel produced, but that the relative proportions of pig iron and scrap used vary considerably between the processes. Because of the high price of pig iron relative to that for scrap, this causes substantial differences between the processes in the unit cost of raw materials.

The table shows the BOS to have the highest unit raw material costs. Unit costs are lowest for the electric arc furnace, but the advantages of the technique are exaggerated. At the time to which the data relate (1971) scrap prices in the UK were held below the world level through an agreement between the steel makers and the scrap suppliers. Under this a maximum price was fixed for the supply of scrap ($31 a ton in 1970), but the merchants purchased at the prevailing (and fluctuating) market prices. Consequently their profit margins were reduced when the demand for scrap (and its price) were high, and were increased when the demand was relatively low. In addition, the Government regulated exports of scrap when domestic demand was high. This arrangement had the advantage for the steelmakers of a steady supply of relatively cheap scrap,[1] but for the scrap merchants, faced with persistently rising costs and a fixed selling price, the "swings and roundabouts" agreement made it increasingly difficult for them to maintain profitability.[2] The agreement was examined by the Restrictive Practices Court in 1963 and judgement was given in January 1964. In this, the agreement was found to yield net benefits to steelmakers

1 Development Coordinating Committee, op. cit., 1966, p. 53.

2 'Reasonable Cause for Optimism', by R.S. Boast, Executive Vice-President, British Scrap Federation, *Financial Times*, 8 October 1971, p. 26.

22

Table 11 *Estimated Raw Material Cost per ton of Crude Steel by Type of Process, U.K.*

	BOS			Open Hearth Cold Metal(b)			Open Hearth Hot Metal(d)			Electric Arc		
	Tons/ton of Crude Steel	Price/ ton of material $	Cost/ton of Crude Steel $	Tons/ton of Crude Steel	Price/ ton of material $	Cost/ton of Crude Steel $	Tons/ton of Crude Steel	Price/ ton of material $	Cost/ton of Crude Steel $	Tons/ton of Crude Steel	Price/ ton of material $	Cost/ton of Crude Steel $
Pig Iron(a)	0.77	62.40	48.05	0.27	69.60(c)	18.80	0.88	62.40	54.91	–	–	–
Scrap	0.33	31.20	10.30	0.82	31.20	25.58	0.22	31.2	6.86	1.08	31.2	33.70
Other materials			3.60			3.60			3.60			3.12
Total			61.94			47.98			65.38			36.82

Notes: (a) Pig Iron price includes capital charges on coke ovens, sinter plant, blast furnace, etc.
(b) Minimum estimate.
(c) Higher pig iron price in cold metal open hearth covers cost of casting liquid iron into cold pig.
(d) Maximum estimate

Source: British Steel Corporation

and to their customers through providing lower scrap prices than would be likely to obtain in a free market, given continued Government control over exports.[1] The agreement was terminated in June 1973 by a unilateral decision of the British Steel Corporation, anticipating the application of the competition regulations of the Commission of the European Communities.

Estimates of the unit operating, labour and capital costs for steel production by the three processes in the UK are given in Table 12. The data for the BOS and open hearth refer to existing facilities, while those for the electric arc furnace are based on engineering information. The BOS facility is a new one, with three vessels each of 300 tons capacity, a configuration which we show below to yield most of the available economies of scale; the open hearth furnace is in a rather older works but has a capacity approaching the estimated optimum.[2] The table shows that even excluding an estimate of administration expenses, the unit conversion costs of steel production via the electric arc furnace route are more than three times those for production via the BOS route, and are substantially greater than for open hearth production. Relating these estimates to the raw material costs of Table 11 gives the following total unit costs:

Open Hearth (Hot Metal)	$78.46
BOS	$68.06
Open Hearth (Cold Metal)	$61.06
Electric Arc	$55.73

Two factors must be borne in mind in interpreting these results. Firstly, the low cost of the open hearth process using cold metal is misleading, since the conversion cost estimates refer to an existing plant and as a result seriously underestimate the capital charges which would prevail in a new facility. Secondly, the unit raw material costs for the electric arc furnace process are based on UK prices prevailing in 1970 which were artificially low as a consequence of the steel scrap agreement. In a free market in which the total quantity of scrap is limited, increasing use of the electric arc process would raise the price of scrap until the total costs of the process tended to equal those of the BOS for comparable steel qualities. Taking account of these two factors would raise the unit production costs for the open hearth process using cold metal above that for the BOS, and would move those for the electric arc process closer to the cost of the BOS.

The major technological advances which led to the emergence of the BOS route as the preferred technique for large-scale crude steel production were the development of the large oxygen converter and increases in the size of blast furnaces. In the oxygen converter, the cycle time is reduced dramatically as compared with the earlier open hearth process (from eight hours to about 45 minutes: in Japan 30 minutes is now being achieved), and the maximum feasible size of converters has

---

1 Registrar of Restrictive Practices, *Restrictive Trading Agreements,* Report of the Registrar, 1 July 1963–30 June 1966 (London: HMSO), Cmnd. 3188, 1966, Agreement between the British Iron and Steel Federation and the National Federation of Scrap Iron, Steel and Metal Merchants, pp. 19–22.

2 The sources and extent of the economies of scale in the main steel-making processes are discussed in Section VII below.

Table 12 *Estimated Crude Steel Production Costs (net of raw material) per ton of annual output by Type of Process, U.K.*

Cost Item	Basic Oxygen System		Open Hearth		Electric Arc	
	$ per ton	%	$ per ton	%	$ per ton	%
Operating labour	0.17	2.7	1.58	12.1		
Maintenance labour	0.10	1.6	1.49	11.4	17.52	92.6
Supplies and Services	0.74	12.2	2.71	20.7		
Maintenance materials	0.79	12.9	0.67	5.1		
Refractories	0.60	9.8	3.10	23.7		
Departmental Works Administrative expenses	2.23	36.5	3.02	23.1	n.a.	n.a.
Depreciation	1.49	24.3	0.50	3.9	1.39	7.4
Total production costs	6.12	100.0	13.08	100.0	18.91	100.0
Size of vessel (tons)	300		240		130	
Weekly Output/Vessel (tons)	60,000		3,300		5,200	

Sources: The data for B.O.S. and Open Hearth facilities are standard costings for existing plants and were supplied by the British Steel Corporation. The electric furnace costs are estimates for a new facility assumed to comprise two furnaces of 30 tons standing capacity and which together produce 0.5 million tons annually (on the basis of 40 taps per furnace per week and a 48 week working year). They have been derived using formulae given in A.H. Leckie, and A.J. Morris, *Effect of Plant and Works Scale on Costs in the Iron and Steel Industry*, Journal of the Iron and Steel Institute, May 1968 pp. 442–448, which were based on actual cost information relating to the British steel industry in the mid-1960s and which we have adjusted to allow for the effects of subsequent inflation. The total capital cost of the electric furnace installation has been calculated using the formula:

$$K = (n. 49400 M^{\frac{2}{3}} + 108 Q + 2640 Q^{\frac{2}{3}}) i$$

where K = total capital cost in £

n = number of furnaces in the installation (in this case 2)

M = vessel standing capacity in tons, and in this case has a value of 130 tons.

Q = weekly throughput of installation (two furnaces) in tons, and has a value of 10,415 tons.

and i = an inflation multiplier with a value in this case of 1.16.

Depreciation cost per annual ton of output has been calculated on the assumption that the facility is written-off simply over 20 years (i.e. depreciation is 5 per cent annually).

Operating cost has been calculated using: $R_Q = \left(\dfrac{n.\,108{,}000}{Q} + 96 \right) i$

where: R_Q = the operating cost per ton of throughput in shillings; n and Q have the same definitions and values as above; i has the same definition as above and a value of 1.25.

25

been steadily increased. To match the increased rate of crude steel output, advances in blast furnace technology were necessary, and as noted above, the size of furnaces has increased substantially in recent years. Oxygen converters need large supplies of hot pig iron at the start of each cycle, and this is provided more easily by increases in the size of individual blast furnaces than by duplicating smaller ones, owing to the difficulties in channelling run-off which are encountered with multi-furnace configurations. The emergence of large-scale works was aided further by increases in the size of rolling mills and in the range of product sizes which they can accomodate.

While such steelworks are suitable for the production of the majority of the steel output of the countries of the enquiry, several factors have operated to increase the absolute quantity of steel, and its share in total output, produced in each country by the semi-integrated electric arc furnace route. The process accounts for the bulk of the production of high-quality special steel, which requires small-scale manufacture using cold scrap. Recently the output of steel by the route has grown rapidly through the production of common grade bars and rods. In the US, for example, more than 40 such 'mini-mills' were constructed during the 1960s.

The circumstances under which mini-mill operation is feasible have been reviewed by W.F. Cartwright.[1] One of the principal factors leading to an expansion of production via this route was the increase in the supply of scrap as the BOS system developed in importance. Oxygen converters use a scrap charge of only 25 to 30 per cent of their burden, as compared with rates of up to 50 per cent in the open-hearth furnace. The effect of this increased supply of scrap was to keep scrap prices relatively stable during the 1960s despite sharp increases in steel output. However, the profitability of mini-mills is very sensitive to the price of scrap: the rise in scrap prices in the US during 1968 caused several mini-mills to close. This sensitivity sets a limit to the amount of steel which can be made by the electric arc furnace route in each country, for as scrap becomes scarce, its price rises. The supply of scrap to electric arc furnaces depends in part upon the proportion absorbed in the BOS; oxygen converters can tolerate scrap proportions of between 15 and 35 per cent. At the lower ratio Cartwright estimates that electric arc furnace steel could form as much as one-third of the UK annual output. With the higher ratio, the proportion would be below one-fifth.[2]

The opportunity to reduce total transport costs has also been an incentive in the construction of mini-mills. Markets for finished steel products are areas which generate considerable volumes of scrap, and short hauls of both scrap and finished products can be obtained.

Cartwright lists further cost savings which can be obtained in mini-mills as compared with large scale works. Closer process control can raise both quality and finished product yields from liquid steel. Many overhead costs, including those of ancilliary works and research and development, can be avoided. Capital costs per ton of annual capacity are also lower in a mini-mill. Iron production facilities are not required and the development of continuous casting and limitation of the product range to bars and rods avoids the need for large scale rolling mills. Construction

1 W.F. Cartwright, *The Place of Mini Steelworks in the World*, Hatfield Memorial Lecture (London: British Steel Corporation), mimeo., 1971.

2 Ibid., Fig. 13.

times for mini-mills are much shorter than for integrated BOS plants (18 months to two years as compared with three years or more), and the equipment is standardised and less technically advanced. As a consequence, returns on investment are obtained more quickly and more certainly.[1]

(c) International Differences in Costs

Table 13 analyses the composition of the value of gross output in U.S. $ for iron and steel production in the countries of the study (with the exception of Canada for which data are unavailable). Great care is necessary in interpreting the results because the data are drawn from a variety of sources and there are differences between the countries in the range of activities to which they relate.[2] However, we are confident that the data for each individual country are internally consistent since in each case they are drawn from a single source, and the results for the EEC are also fairly consistent between the member countries as they were obtained from the first community-wide census of production.[3]

The second column for each country shows the values of gross output and its components per ton of crude steel produced. These results should be taken only as indicating the broad orders of magnitude for each nation, since variations will occur because of differences in the importance of crude steel production in the overall activities of the industry, differences in factor and product prices, and inconsistencies in the data as well as through differences in efficiency levels. Gross output per ton varies widely between the countries. The highest value occurs in the Netherlands, where it is almost twice that for Belgium-Luxembourg, which has the lowest value. The US has a relatively high unit gross output value, while three countries (France, Germany, F.R., and the UK) are grouped towards the middle of this range. The differences are the product of the net variations between the countries in the components of gross output. We cannot hope fully to explain these variations, but we can examine the major features which appear likely to influence them.

Raw materials: The table shows the purchases of raw materials, etc., per unit of crude steel output to differ substantially between the countries, forming between 52 and 69 per cent of gross output. The chief factors which may affect these variations are the degree of vertical integration in each industry (*ceteris paribus* the greater the integration the lower will be the raw material purchases), the range of products produced (some require zinc and tin in the finishing processes), the prices of the raw materials, and the proportions in which they are combined together. The latter two items are of particular importance for our enquiry since variations in the costs of raw materials per unit of crude steel output which are independent of the level of production may affect the significance of economies of scale.

1   Ibid., p. 13 and Figs 15 and 16. Cartwright notes that with scrap prices prevailing in the UK in 1971, the DCF rate of return over 15 years was higher on mini-mills than on integrated BOS plants.

2   These differences are indicated in the footnotes to the table.

3   Office Statistique des Communautés Européenes, *Resultats Définitifs de l'Enquête Industrielle de 1963*, Etudes Statistiques, No. 2, (Brussels) 1969.

Table 13 Absolute and Percentage Distribution of Gross Output by Components, Iron and Steel Production by Country, 1963 (Japan 1965)

	Belgium-Luxembourg(a)			France(a)			Germany, F.R.(a)			Italy(a)			Netherlands(a)		
	$m	$/ton	%	$m	$/ton	%	$m	$/ton	%	$m	$/ton	%	$m	$/ton	%
Gross output	1333.1	115.4	100.0	2976.6	169.5	100.0	5029.2	159.2	100.0	1345.5	132.5	100.0	504.5	215.4	100.0
purchases of raw materials and goods for resale, payments for purchases received	779.2	67.4	58.5	1705.7	97.2	57.3	2661.0	84.2	52.9	779.4	76.7	57.9	269.6	115.1	53.4
Net Output	553.9	47.9	41.5	1270.9	72.4	42.7	2368.2	75.0	47.1	566.1	55.7	42.1	234.9	100.3	46.6
wages and salaries	260.2	22.5	19.5	473.0	26.9	15.9	1030.7-	32.6	20.5	145.6	14.3	10.8	70.4	30.1	14.0
other	293.7	25.4	22.0	797.9	45.4	26.8	1337.5	42.3	26.6	420.5	41.4	31.3	164.5	70.2	32.6
depreciation															
net trading profit before tax															
residue															
Total output of crude steel ('000 tons)	11,556			17,557			31,597			10,157			2,342		

	E.E.C.(a)			U.K.(c)			U.S.A.(b)			Canada			Japan(d)		
	$m	$/ton	%	$m	$/ton	%	$m	$/ton	%				$m	$/ton	%
Gross output	11188.9	152.8	100.0	3686.2	161.1	100.0	19146.1(g,h)	193.2	100.0				4664.4	148.0	100.0
purchases of raw materials and goods for resale, payments for purchases received	6194.7	84.6	55.4	2551.3	111.5	69.2	10570.5(h)	106.6	55.2		data not available		3198.6	101.5	68.6
Net Output	4994.1	68.2	44.6	1134.9	49.6	30.8	8617.3(i)	86.9	45.0				1465.7	46.5	31.4
wages and salaries	1979.9	27.0	17.7	681.3(e)	29.8	18.5	4167.9	42.0	21.8				633.1	20.1	13.6
other	3014.2	41.2	26.9	386.3	16.9	10.5	4449.4	44.9	23.2				832.5	26.4	17.8
depreciation				224.9(f)	9.8	6.1							301.9(d)	9.6	6.5
net trading profit before tax				114.3	5.0	3.1							150.8	4.8	3.2
residue				114.5	5.0	3.1							379.8(k)	12.1	8.1
Total output of crude steel ('000 tons)	73,209			22,881			99,121						31,509		

Notes:

(a) Data refer to iron and steel production, excluding rolling, finishing and tube manufacture: Group 351 of the "Nomenclature des Industries établies dans les Communautés européenes" (N.I.C.E.)

(b) Data refer to S.I.C. Group 331 (Blast Furnaces, Steel Works and Rolling and Finishing).

(c) Data refer to M.L.H. 311 (Iron and steel (General)); included are iron and steel production, rolling and finishing, but not tube manufacture.

(d) Data are for 1965 and refer to manufacture of all iron and steel products.

(e) Includes employers' contributions to National Insurance, etc.

(f) Capital allowances for tax.

(g) Value of shipments.

(h) Contain extensive duplication because of inter-establishment shipments.

(i) Adjusted for changes in stocks; hence with purchases of raw materials, etc (which are unadjusted) does not sum to value of shipments.

(j) Depreciation.

(k) Of which interest = $296.4m.

Sources: (i) Financial data: — E.E.C. and members: Office Statistique des Communautés Européennes, *Résultats Définitifs de l'enquête Industrielle de 1963*, op. cit. 1969.

-U.S.: Bureau of the Census, *Census of Manufactures, 1963*, Volume II, Industry Statistics, Part II, (Washington DC: US Government Printing Office) 1966.

-U.K.: Board of Trade, *Report on the Census of Production for 1963*, Part 37 (London: H.M.S.O.) 1966.

-Japan: Japan Iron and Steel Federation, *Statistical Yearbook 1971*, (Tokyo) 1971.

(ii) Output Data: British Steel Corporation, *Statistical Handbook 1971, 1968.*

So far as we are able to judge, however, prices do not in general vary greatly between countries, and the effect of such differences as are apparent is probably not too great. With respect to *iron ore*, in recent years ample supplies together with increases in the size of bulk-ore carrying ships have exercised a fairly steady downward influence on prices, and have kept competitive pressures high. As a consequence the delivered price of ore of a specified grade does not appear to differ greatly between the countries. Most of the countries of the enquiry are substantial net importers of ore, the two exceptions being France and Canada which are well-endowed with deposits and are net exporters. In 1967 the average landed price of high-quality Swedish ore to the EEC countries was $9.39 per ton,[1] and prices for comparable qualities elsewhere were probably similar. One feature which is likely to induce some variation between the countries in the costs of their ore purchases is the quality of their handling and distribution facilities. For example, delivered prices of imported ore in the UK probably tend to be elevated slightly above the world average because of the present lack of deepwater docks to accomodate large carriers and the absence of tidewater steelworks.

Within the EEC, the secular downward trend in prices seems also to have been reflected in the price of *pig iron*, and it is likely that this tendency has been present in the remaining countries. Data from the EEC Commission for the member countries and the UK show that there are some inter-country differences in the levels of home prices of haematite pig iron for steel-making. The four-year average prices for the period ended 1968 cluster around $67.00 per ton for Belgium-Luxembourg, France, the Netherlands and the UK, and are $57.35 and $60.80 for Germany, F.R. and Italy respectively.[2] We have no comparable data for the North American countries and Japan. The inter-country differences are greater if the costs of hot metal — which is required in the BOS — are considered. These variations reflect the labour and capital cost differences which we discuss below.

Home *scrap* prices show rather more variation between the countries. The four-year average price to 1968 was lowest for France ($24.81 per ton), highest for Italy ($38.00) and between $29.00 and $31.00 for the remaining countries (with the exception of Canada and Japan, for which comparable data are not available).[3]

Since pig iron is the largest raw material component in steel manufacture via the BOS (see Table 11), the broadly similar levels of its price in the various countries reduces the impact of the wider variations in scrap prices upon the unit materials costs in crude steel production, and for the purposes of this study we may regard international differences in unit raw material costs in the BOS as being insignificant.[4]

1 Office Statistique des Communautés Européennes, *Sidérurgie*, (Brussels), 1968, Table II–54A, p. 342.

2 Ibid., Table II–58, p. 352.

3 Ibid., Table II–63, p. 357.

4 Assuming pig iron and scrap inputs per ton of crude steel produced in the BOS to be as given in Table 11 we calculated the unit raw material costs in the EEC countries and the UK using the data from Office Statistique des Communautés Européennes, op. cit., 1968. Costs were about $60.00 per ton, with the exception of Germany, F.R., where low home prices of both pig iron and scrap reduced total unit costs to about $54.00 (or 90 per cent of the costs in the other countries).

However, the higher price of pig iron as compared with that for scrap in each country does mean that nations in which pig iron intensive techniques of steel production are relatively more important suffer some raw material cost disadvantage. In 1968, Belgium-Luxembourg and France had very high pig iron to scrap ratios (of 80 and 70 per cent respectively) as a result of the importance of the Basic Bessemer process in each. By contrast Italy employed only slightly above 40 per cent of pig iron, indicating the relative importance of the electric arc and open-hearth processes.[1] As the wider introduction of the BOS continues, raw material cost differences associated with variations in production techniques will tend to disappear, and we may discount this factor in our subsequent analysis.

Employment Costs: Table 13 shows wages and salaries per ton of crude steel output to be highest in the US, with the costs for the other countries ranging between 78 per cent (for Germany, F.R.) and 34 per cent (for Italy) of the US figures. We have indicated above that these results may be misleading owing to differences between the industries in the nature and range of activities they undertake. Because of this we have attempted to indicate the inter-country variations in direct employment costs per ton of crude steel output, to analyse the contributions to these variations of differences in productivity and earnings, and to examine the recent trends in each of these variables.

Table 14 shows unit direct employment costs for each country in 1967, and also (with the exception of Canada) productivity per man-hour and average hourly earnings. The table indicates that unit employment costs are highest in the US, the UK and Canada, and are less than half the US level in the EEC countries and Japan. Productivity is shown to be close to, or somewhat above the US level in the EEC countries and Japan, but is very low in the UK. Average hourly earnings are considerably below those in the US for all countries for which data are available. However extreme care must be exercised in interpreting the significance of these results for the steel industry at the present moment, both because differences between the nations in the compilation of the basic data introduce a substantial degree of bias, and because the table relates to 1967. With regard to the first factor, the industry definitions for the UK and Japan are much wider than for the EEC, and the results for France may be influenced by the importance of mining in that country's steel industry. In Japan earnings are probably underestimated because of the extensive provision of fringe benefits, and productivity over-gauged because of the practice of contracting out for certain classes of labour, particularly for maintenance. The age of the data is important because subsequent productivity increases in Japan may have further improved its unit labour cost position relative to the other nations.

Even allowing for these qualifications the implication of the results for 1967 is clear. The US, and presumably to a lesser extent Canada, are high labour cost countries because of high average earnings. The advantage of the EEC countries and to some extent also Japan lies in their relatively low earnings levels. The disadvantage of the UK is the product of its very low productivity rating coupled with a high level of earnings. Unfortunately, data for 1973, which would show substantial changes, are not yet available.

1   British Steel Corporation, *Statistical Handbook 1968* (London) 1969.

Table 14 *Productivity, Hourly Earnings and Unit Employment Costs, Iron and Steel Production, by Country, 1967*

Country	Crude Steel Output per Man-Hour		Average Hourly Earnings		Employment Cost per unit of Crude Steel Output (1/col. 2 × col. 3)	
	tons	Index	$US	Index	$US	Index
Belgium-Luxembourg	0.106	100	1.39	38	13.07	39
France	0.083	78	0.88	24	10.57	31
Germany, F.R.	0.111	105	1.32	37	11.93	35
Italy	0.139	131	0.98	27	7.07	21
Netherlands	0.155	146	1.33	37	8.60	25
E.E.C.	0.107	101	1.16	32	10.83	32
U.K.	0.037	35	1.25	35	33.97	100
U.S.	0.106	100	3.62	100	33.99	100
Canada	n.a.	n.a.	n.a.	n.a.	29.66	87
Japan	0.081	76	0.95	26	11.75	35

Source: Output data: BSC, *Statistical Handbook 1969*, op. cit.
Employment and Earnings data:
EEC – Office Statistique des Communautés Européennes, *Sidérurgie*, (Brussels), 1968.
UK – BSC, *Annual Statistics* 1969, (London), 1970
US – American Iron and Steel Institute, *Annual Statistical Report, 1969*, (Washington DC), 1970.
Canada – BSC, *Statistical Handbook 1969*, op. cit.
Japan – Japan Iron and Steel Federation, *Statistical Yearbook, 1971*, (Tokyo), 1971.

The trends in productivity, earnings, and unit employment costs between 1960 and 1967 are indicated in Table 15. Again caution in required in interpretation. Productivity grew very slowly in the UK, while it increased by one-half, on average in the EEC, and was up two-and-one-half times in Japan. Earnings increased slightly faster than productivity in the EEC as a whole, causing unit labour costs also to rise, the effect being most noticeable in the Netherlands. Earnings advancing ahead of productivity also contributed to a rise in unit labour costs in the UK. In Japan and the US productivity increased at a greater rate than earnings, causing unit labour costs actually to fall over the period. With the exception of Japan, the tendency was for unit labour cost differentials relative to the US to narrow.

Capital Costs: The data in Table 13 are only sufficiently disaggregated to provide an indication of the magnitude of capital charges (as indicated by depreciation) in the UK, and no international comparisons on the basis of census information are possible. Even if they were, very little confidence could be placed in them, since the definition and methods of calculation of depreciation differ between the countries and the industries vary also in their range of activities and in the age-distribution of their capital stocks.

We have been able to find very little evidence on the extent of international differences in capital costs in the steel industry. Such as exists suggests there are considerable differences between Japan and the Western nations. The Fukuyama complex of Nippon KKK, designed to produce 12 million tons of crude steel

Table 15 *Indices of Productivity, Hourly Earnings and Unit Employment Costs, Iron and Steel Production, by Country, 1960, 1965, 1967 (1960 = 100)*

Country and Year	Crude Steel Output per Man-Hour	Average Hourly Earnings	Employment Cost per Unit of Crude Steel Output
Belgium-Luxembourg			
1960	100	100	100
1965	127	136	108
1967	143	153	106
France			
1960	100	100	100
1965	124	138	111
1967	143	152	105
Germany, F.R.			
1960	100	100	100
1965	118	146	126
1967	139	157	114
Italy			
1960	100	100	100
1965	145	163	113
1967	189	182	97
Netherlands			
1960	100	100	100
1965	133	171	129
1967	146	202	138
E.E.C.			
1960	100	100	100
1965	125	143	116
1967	149	157	107
U.K.			
1960	100	100	100
1965	119	135	113
1967[a]	116	128	112
U.S.			
1960	100	100	100
1965	124	112	90
1967	128	118	91
Canada			
1960			
1965	n.a.	n.a.	n.a.
1967			
Japan			
1960	100	100	100
1965	175	152	87
1967	253	190	75

Notes: (a) Change in basis of employment and earnings data, indices not strictly comparable with earlier years.

Sources: as for Table 14.

annually, is costing an estimated $1,400 million, or $108 per ton of annual capacity.[1] By contrast, a study for the Commission of the EEC suggests that a new integrated works to produce 7 to 8 million tons of crude steel a year would cost $1,600 million, or $229 per ton of annual capacity.[2] Pratten identifies variations in the level of general efficiency (i.e. X — efficiency) as a factor contributing to higher rates of output in Japan as compared with the UK and the US when identical plants are considered,[3] and this clearly suggests lower capital costs per ton of crude steel produced in Japan. Capital charges may also differ because of variations in the capital-labour ratio and because of differences in the quality of plants.

There is rather more evidence to suggest that the capital costs of process plant differ internationally, and it seems likely that comparable variations may be expected in the steel industry. Burn has collated estimates of the capital costs of large, broadly comparable, plants in the chemical industry since 1959 for the countries of our own enquiry with the exception of Belgium-Luxembourg.[4] He finds that during the period costs in the US were generally slightly above those in Western Europe and Japan; at most the difference was 25 per cent and usually it was much less. UK costs, while below those in the US were substantially above those in the countries of Western Europe and Japan. The small international cost disadvantage of the US results from the fact that its high relative labour productivity level does not quite entirely offset its high relative wages. Burn indicates that if the rate of return on capital is assumed equal between the countries and if in each price is equal to the plant capital cost per unit of capacity, the competitive impact of the cost differential will be very slight.

Of more importance is the finding that the length of time taken for the construction of process plants varies between the countries.[5] The fastest building rates are achieved by the US and Japan with slightly lower rates in continental Western Europe. Construction times are very much longer in the UK, where they are between $2\frac{1}{2}$ and 3 years, as compared with an average of perhaps 15 months in the world as a whole.[6] Similar differences appear to exist when commissioning periods are considered. In the UK periods of between 3 to 4 years are usual for new plants to be run up to planned capacity, whereas in Japan facilities are brought fully onstream in perhaps half this time. When a discounted cash flow method of appraisal

1 *33 Magazine*, November 1971.

2 Commission des Communautés Européennes, *Projet de Memorandum sur les objectifs généraux de la Sidérurgie de la Communauté pour les années 1975–80*, (mimeo), 31 March 1971.

3 C.F. Pratten, op. cit. 1971, pp. 106–7.

4 D. Burn, *Chemicals Under Free Trade* (London: The Atlantic Trade Study), 1971, pp. 82–9

5 Ibid.

6 National Economic Development Office, *Investment in the Process Industries* Second report of the Process Plant Working Party, (London, H.M.S.O.), 1967 p. 12.

is employed, increases in the length of construction and commissioning times seriously affect the profitability of the new investment.[1]

While these findings suggest fairly strongly that there are substantial variations between countries in the steel industry, it is impossible to give any quantitative indication, and in our subsequent analysis of necessity we assume capital charges to be identical in each country.

Prices: International variations in the value of gross output will also result from differences between countries in the average prices charged for particular products and in the combination of goods of different prices which are sold. The average price for a specified product depends upon the weighted contribution of domestic and export prices. Appendix 3 gives details of the published domestic prices of selected classes of finished steel products as at 1 May 1971 in the UK, the members of the EEC and the US. The data are adjusted for rebates insofar as these are notified by the producers and are permitted by official regulations and other agreements. However, secret discounts on published prices, either to all purchasers or to selected customers, are probably important, particularly when demand is slack, and the data may be misleading, therefore, on this account. Within each product class there are substantial differences between the countries in the prices charged, but these differences do not remain wholly consistent between the classes. In 15 out of 16 cases in which a comparison can be made, the US charges the highest domestic prices, but the rankings of the other nations vary considerably. Prices of exports are generally below those charged in the domestic market, and they tend to fluctuate more sharply with the steel cycle. Other things equal, the larger is the proportion of a country's

1   The impact of a delay can be illustrated by a simple example of a project with an initial investment cost of $1000 and an expected life of ten years. The table below shows that without a construction delay, at a discount rate of 10 per cent the net present value of the project is zero (i.e. the discounted cash inflow over the life of the project is just equal to the initial cost). With a two-year delay, ignoring interest charges on the investment during the delay and assuming the same cash flow profile, the net present value is − $172. The internal rate of return falls to 6.3 per cent.

Effect of a Construction Delay on the Profitability of Capital Project

Year	Cash Flow		Present Value Factors at 10% Discount Rate	Net Cash Flow	
	Undelayed	Delayed		Undelayed	Delayed
0	−1000	−1000	1.0000	−1000	−1000
1	235	0	0.9091	214	0
2	235	0	0.8264	194	0
3	212	235	0.7513	159	177
4	189	235	0.6830	129	161
5	161	212	0.6209	100	132
6	140	189	0.5645	79	107
7	113	161	0.5132	58	83
8	81	140	0.4665	38	65
9	47	113	0.4241	20	48
10	24	81	0.3855	9	31
11	−	47	0.3505	−	16
12	−	24	0.3186	−	8
			Net Present Value	0	−172

output going to export, the lower will be its average product price. The differential between domestic and export prices occurs in large part because producers are able to discriminate between their home and foreign markets. The price elasticity of demand for steel products is lower over that part of the domestic market in which the indigenous manufacturers have relatively large monopoly powers as a result of their proximity to their customers and their knowledge of demand than in the export sectors of markets abroad. In these conditions, profits are maximised where a level of output is produced which sets the combined marginal revenue from the two markets (summed horizontally) equal to total marginal cost, and where this output is allocated between the markets such that marginal revenue is equal in each. Given that demand elasticities differ, this implies different prices in each market.

Frequently the practice of exporting industries of selling abroad at a lower price than at home raises the charge of dumping (usually from the domestic industry which is suffering from imports). Dumping is a special case of price discrimination in which the profit-maximising price in the export market is below the total average unit cost for the producing industry. Steel seems particularly susceptible to this because of the wide gap between total costs and variable costs (on account of high capital intensity) and because of its chronic tendency to develop surplus capacity. This occurs both as demand levels decline cyclically and as new capacity has to be added in large indivisible lumps. Dumping is very difficult to prove in practice and is easily (and sometimes conveniently) confused with the overall price advantage which a foreign producer may have as a result of greater efficiency or lower factor costs. The latter case probably goes a considerable way towards explaining the increase in the penetration of Japanese steel into the US market in recent years.[1]

Average price levels will also be higher the greater is the representation of relatively high-priced products in the total sales of a country. Very broadly, the prices per ton of flat-rolled products are below those of the other classes of goods, and this will tend to reduce the value of gross output in those countries in which these products are predominant (see Table 2).[2]

1 Cf. American Iron and Steel Institute, *The Steel Problem,*(New York), 1968, and Committee on Finance, U.S. Senate, op. cit., 1967

2 See C.K. Rowley, *Steel and Public Policy,* (London: McGraw-Hill), 1971, p. 102.

V

Average Plant and Firm Sizes

The obvious starting point for a comparison of the structures of the steel industries is a consideration of the average sizes of plants and firms. We gauge size in terms of estimated annual crude steelmaking capacity; the data have been obtained from an international directory of iron and steel producers[1] and exclude units without steel-making facilities (for example, non-integrated ironworks, foundries and re-rolling mills). The methods used to derive the estimates are described in Appendix 4.

The simplest way to calculate the averages is to divide total industry capacity by the total number of firms or plants in operation. However, in comparing differences in relative sizes between countries this may produce misleading results. This is because whilst the size distribution of plants and firms in most industries is assy-metrically skewed towards the upper end, producing a "tail" of small units, the length and importance of this tail may differ, and critically affect comparisons of mean plant and firm size. The "tail" typically includes those producers who are in the process of expanding to larger scales, those who are declining and will eventually leave the industry, and those who cater to specialist or localised markets. The latter are of some importance in most steel industries, and are represented by semi-integrated units employing electric arc technology and producing either common grade bars and rods or high-quality special steels.

In his pioneering international comparison of plant and firm sizes, Bain[2] endeavoured to overcome the problem of the "tail" by calculating the mean size by employment of the twenty largest plants and firms in each industry in each of the countries of his sample. However, as Scherer[3] has recently pointed out, this still produces a biased result, since taking a finite number of the largest units in each industry will incorporate progressively more of the tail of the distribution the smaller is the size of the industry, and the smaller is the number of total units.

An attractive solution, originated by Scherer,[4] is to calculate the average size of the largest plants or firms accounting for a specified percentage of the total size of

---

1 H.G. and G. Cordero (eds.), *Iron and Steelworks of the World*, (London: Metal Bulletin Books Ltd), 1957 and 1969.

2 J.S. Bain, op. cit., 1966.

3 F.M. Scherer, *The Economics of Multi-Plant Operation: An International Comparisons Study*, with A. Beckstein, E. Kaufer, and R.D. Murphy, (Cambridge, Mass.: Harvard University Press), forthcoming.

4 F.M. Scherer, op. cit.

Table 16 *Average Capacities of Plants and Firms contributing two-thirds of Total Crude Steel Capacity, mid-1950s and late-1960s, by Country*

(a) Plants	Average Capacity				Index of Capacity increase
Country	mid-1950s		late-1960s		
	m. tons	% of US.	m. tons	% of US.	[col.4/col.2 × 100]
Belgium-Luxembourg	0.76	30	1.85	36	243
France	1.02	41	1.70	33	167
Germany F.R.	n.a.	n.a.	2.72	53	n.a.
Italy	0.46	18	1.96	39	426
Netherlands	n.a.	n.a.	2.37	47	n.a.
U.K.	1.00	40	1.59	31	159
U.S.	2.51	100	5.08	100	202
Canada	1.31	52	2.56	50	194
Japan	0.68	27	4.71	93	693

(b) Firms	Average Capacity				Index of Capacity increase
	mid-1950s		late-1960s		
	m. tons	% of US.	m. tons	% of US.	[col.4/col.2 × 100]
Belgium-Luxembourg	1.36	15	3.69	21	271
France	1.78	19	6.80	38	382
Germany F.R.	n.a.	n.a.	5.98	34	n.a.
Italy	0.65	7	3.93	22	605
Netherlands	n.a.	n.a.	2.37	13	n.a.
U.K.	1.67	18	3.57	20	214
U.S.	9.40	100	17.78	100	189
Canada	1.31	14	2.56	14	195
Japan	1.36	15	11.77	66	865

Source: H.G. and G. Cordero (eds.), op. cit., 1957 and 1969

the industry (measured by output, capacity, employment, etc.). In this way the average size of the major units can be compared, irrespective of the size of the industry or the number of units. For our study of the steel industry, we have compared the average sizes of the largest plants and firms contributing two-thirds of total crude steel capacity in the mid-1950s and in the late-1960s. The results are displayed in Table 16.

The first part of the table presents the results for plants. In the late-1960s, average plant size was largest in the US and Japan, and was almost twice that in the countries with the next largest plants (Canada and Germany, F.R.). A comparison with Table 1 shows that there is a strong connection between the size of the industry and the mean plant size.[1] During the period since the mid-1950s mean plant size has increased in every country for which data are available, with the greatest rate of increase occuring in Japan. Firms are analysed in the second part of the table. For both periods, the dispersion of average firm sizes relative to that for the US is greater than when plants are considered; the sole exception being France in the late-1960s. Except for Canada and the US, the rate of increase in average firm size between the mid-1950s and the late-1960s was greater than for plants, indicating an increase in multi-plant operation.

1 The simple coefficient of correlation is + 0.9.

VI

The Structure of Production

In this section we review the recent trends in the structure and performance of the steel industry in each country of the sample. A note on the overall developments in the European Economic Community is also included.

(a) Belgium-Luxembourg

Within the EEC, the steel industry of Belgium-Luxembourg grew at a below average 5.0 per cent in the period between 1950 and 1969 (Table 1). In 1970, it produced 18.1 million tons of crude steel (or 17 per cent of the total EEC output), of which 12.6 million tons were made in Belgium and the remainder in Luxembourg.[1] Until the mid-1960s, when it was passed by Japan, the industry was the largest steel exporter by volume of the countries of the enquiry, and currently ships abroad 90 per cent of its annual output. About two-thirds of exports are to other countries of the EEC. The financial performance of the Belgian industry (comparable data for Luxembourg are not available) varied considerably during the 1960s, falling from a rate of return on capital employed of 8.1 per cent in 1960, to 0.8 per cent in 1966, before rising to 7.2 per cent in 1970. The annual average for the period was a moderate 3.5 per cent.[2] Because of the importance of exports, the profitability of the industry is very sensitive to variations in the world level of prices. Despite the fluctuations in, and low overall level of, profitability, investment per ton of crude steel output was fairly high in relation to that of most of the other countries, and reached a peak of $22.5 per ton in 1966 (Table 5), the year of lowest profitability. The investment rate was achieved in some measure through Government assistance.

In 1969, the industry comprised 25 producers, of which 9 were integrated companies with pig-iron making facilities, two were semi-integrated firms using open hearth or electric furnaces, and the remaining 14 were re-rolling and finishing concerns.[3] The output rates of the largest producers are shown in Table 17. Both firms and plants exhibit a high degree of product specialisation, and within the industry as a whole, the manufacture of light-rolled common steel products is

1 Economic Commission for Europe, *Quarterly Bulletin of Steel Statistics for Europe,* (New York: United Nations), Vol. 22, No. 1., 1971, Table Ad.

2 Groupement des Hauts Forneaux et Acieries Belges, *La Sidérurgie Belge en 1970,* (Brussels), 1970, p. 45.

3 Comité de la Sidérurgie Belge, *The Belgian Iron and Steel Industry,* (Brussels), 1970, pp. 26–7, and H.G. and G. Cordero (eds.), op. cit., 1969.

Table 17 *Belgium-Luxembourg: Crude Steel Production by, and Shares in National Output of,*
Major Steel Companies, 1970 (1969)

Company	Crude Steel Production (million tons)	Share in National Output (%)
Cockerill	5.19[a]	28.7
Arbed (Luxembourg)	4.96[b]	27.4
Sidmar[c]	1.83	10.1
Metallurgique Hainaut-Sambre	1.80	10.0
Thy-Marcinelle et Monceau	1.34	7.4
Clabecq	0.83	4.6
Fabrique de Fer	0.40	2.2
Total of 7 largest producers	16.35	90.5
Others	1.72	9.5
Total	18.07[d]	100.0

Notes: (a) excludes output of 1.0 million tons from French works.
  (b) 1969 production; excludes output of 1.25 million tons from Saar (Germany) works.
  (c) Arbed have a 48 per cent interest; Cockerill a 30 per cent interest.
  (d) 1970 total, from Economic Commission for Europe, op. cit., 1971.
Sources: B.S.C. data for Arbed; remainder from Comité de la Sidérurgie Belge.

important (Table 2). Only the two major companies, Cockerill of Belgium and Arbed of Luxembourg manufacture a full range of products: the other steel manufacturers concentrate on narrower ranges of flat or light-rolled products. The production of special steels forms about 10 per cent of total output, and is virtually entirely accounted for by Allegheny-Longdoz, a company jointly owned by Cockerill and Allegheny-Ludlum, the major US special steel producer. Specialisation at plant level is high, with individual works generally concentrating on one of the major product groups.

Integration beyond the normal iron and steel-making activities is not highly developed. An important feature of the industry is the continued existence of the independent re-rollers, the majority of whose output goes to export. The reasons for the survival of these is not clear, but one possible explanation is that they are prepared to undertake small orders for specified sizes and grades of steel products. Companies do not own ore mines, and have not generally developed activities beyond the stock-holding stage. The exception is Cockerill, which has engineering, steel fabricating and ship-building divisions.

During the past two decades, the numbers of steel-making companies and plants have fallen. *Iron and Steel Works of the World* lists 16 firms and 25 plants in 1956; the comparative figures for 1968 were 10 and 18 respectively.[1] The reduction has been achieved largely through merger, and the impact on the size-distributions of companies and plants is indicated in Table 18. While larger firms and plants have increased in importance, the shares of total capacity for which they account are low in relation to most (though not all) of the other countries of the enquiry. Of the seven nations possessing companies with capacities of 5 million tons or above, only the UK (before nationalisation) had a smaller proportion of total capacity

1 H.G. and G. Cordero (eds.)., op. cit, 1957 and 1969

Table 18 *Belgium-Luxembourg: Distribution of Crude Steelmaking Capacity by Size of Firm and Plant, mid-1950s and late-1960s*

Capacity Range (m. tons)	Percentage of Capacity			
	Firms		Plants	
	mid-1950s	late-1960s	mid-1950s	late-1960s
Below 0.5	17.9	0.6	31.9	0.9
0.5 − 0.9	16.2	2.5	41.7	16.0
1.0 − 1.9	23.7	25.8	26.4	51.1
2.0 − 4.9	42.3	41.2	−	32.0
5.0 and above	−	29.9	−	−
Total	100.0	100.0	100.0	100.0
Total capacity of estimates (m. tons)	10.2	22.2	10.2	22.2

Source: H.G. and G. Cordero (eds.), op. cit., 1957 and 1969. For the method of derivation of the data see Appendix 4.

contained in them (Table 26), and when plants of 2 million tons capacity or above are considered, only in France and the UK (Tables 20 and 26) do they account for lower capacity proportions. The relatively small scale of plant and firms in Belgium-Luxembourg is causing the industry some concern at present, and is one of the major factors which has induced the Belgian Government to provide funds for investment under preferential conditions, since large-scale units are of great importance in an industry which is so heavily dependent upon exports.

The most important series of mergers have been those which have led to the development of the Cockerill group. In 1955, Cockerill acquired two important steel producers, d'Ougrée-Marihaye and de Ferblatil, to form Cockerill-Ougrée. This expanded Cockerill's control over the production of pig iron and steel, and allowed the consolidation of production onto the larger plants of the group. In 1966, Forges de la Providence was absorbed, principally to consolidate and expand the product range. In 1970 Cockerill-Ougrée-Providence acquired the second-largest Belgian producer, Espérance-Longdoz, in order to extend the range of flat-rolled products manufactured. The scope for rationalisation in this case was considerable, since Providence's steel works and mills are located alongside those of Cockerill in Liège, and the reallocation of output among them has enabled longer production runs to be achieved.

The majority of modernisation and rationalisation has been achieved within existing plants. One of the biggest projects involving the construction of new facilities has been the establishment in 1968 of an integrated works with an initial capacity of 2.5 million tons to produce sheet and coil. This development has been undertaken by Sidmar, a company whose major shareholders are Cockerill and Arbed. Because new construction has been a relatively rare event, the vast bulk of Belgium-Luxembourg's steelmaking capacity is located at inland sites, close to the original (though now depleted) coal and iron ore deposits of Liège, Charleroi and the Campine, and this is clearly a problem for an export-oriented industry, which competes with other producers having coastal locations. However, within the industry it is felt that a large part of the competitive advantage of these plants derives from their modernity, and in the course of time, much of this advantage will disappear.

(b) France[1]

In 1971, there were 66 firms in the French iron and steel industry, operating 99 plants (a plant-to-firm ratio of 1.5). The plants included 54 integrated works making both iron and steel, 5 units producing pig-iron only, and 40 re-rolling and finishing works. The numbers of firms and plants have contracted sharply in recent years: in 1965 there were 82 firms operating 118 plants.[2]

Crude steel production is very heavily concentrated on two companies, Wendel-Sidelor and Usinor, which in 1969 produced over 7 million ingot tons each, and together accounted for almost 70 per cent of total industry output. Table 19 gives details for the six largest producers. Only the two major firms manufacture a full range of finished steel products including special steels: the medium and small concerns concentrate upon the production of semis and either flat or light and heavy rolled goods. Thus Chiers, the third largest producer, manufactures mainly strip and wire, while Neuves Maisons Châtillon, ranking fifth by output, produces bars and rods. About 20 companies produce special steel, and this number includes some of

Table 19 *France: Crude Steel Production by, and Share in National Output of, Major Steel Companies, 1969*

Company	Crude Steel Production (million tons)	Share in National Output (%)
Wendel-Sidelor	7.88	35.0
Usinor	7.51	33.3
Chiers	0.83	3.7
Normandie	0.74	3.3
Neuves Maisons Châtillon	0.62	2.8
C.A.F.L.	0.62	2.8
Total of 6 largest producers	18.20	80.9
Others	4.32	19.1
Total	22.52	100.0

Source: B.S.C. data

the larger manufacturers. However, the majority of special steel output comes from small, specialist producers, of which Ugine Kuhlmann, with an estimated capacity of 250,000 ingot tons but ranking third overall in the industry on the basis of turnover, is the largest. In general, therefore, the degree of specialisation in the French industry is probably higher than in several other countries, and this may serve to offset to some extent the relatively small average sizes of firms and plants (Table 16)

1 Much of this section is based upon an interesting discussion with M. Lefèvre of the Chambre Syndicale de la Sidérurgie Française in Paris in September 1971.

2 Chambre Syndicale de la Sidérurgie Française, *La Sidérurgie Française en 1970,* (Paris), 1971, p. 67.

Vertical integration prior to the iron-making stage and after the finishing stage is not a marked feature of the industry. Of the larger firms, some own ore mines, while most provide transport facilities for domestic wholesalers and final consumers. The inclusion of construction and heavy engineering activities in steel firms is unusual, the most notable exception being S.F.A.C. which produces special steels and has a large engineering division.

Table 20 shows that there has been a dramatic change in the structure of the steel industry at the level of the firm in the period since the mid-1950s. At the beginning, there were no companies with crude steel capacities of 5 million tons or above, but by the late-1960s such firms contributed two-thirds of total capacity. This development is attributable entirely to mergers, the most important of which have taken place since 1966 and the effects of which had not been fully reflected at plant level by the end of the decade. Many small plants had been shut down, and others modernised and their productivity improved, but works in the two million tons or above range accounted for only one-quarter of total capacity.

Table 20 *France: Distribution of Crude Steelmaking Capacity by Size of Firm and Plant, mid-1950s and late-1960s*

Capacity Range (m. tons)	Percentage of Capacity			
	Firms		Plants	
	mid-1950s	late-1960s	mid-1950s	late-1960s
Below 0.5	24.2	5.3	36.2	10.8
0.5 − 0.9	9.0	10.5	22.2	19.9
1.0 − 1.9	45.5	9.0	41.7	43.4
2.0 − 4.9	21.4	9.2	−	25.9
5.0 and above	−	66.0	−	−
Total	100.0	100.0	100.0	100.0
Total capacity of estimates (m. tons)	10.6	30.6	10.6	30.6

Source: as for Table 18.

Wendel-Sidelor, the largest producer, was formed in 1968 by the merger of de Wendel and Sidelor, who had previously cooperated to establish a jointly-owned subsidiary, Sacillor to manufacture bars, sections and other light-rolled products. Sidelor itself was the product of an extensive series of mergers in the 1950s. Usinor was formed through mergers prior to 1950, but achieved its present status through the absorption of Lorraine-Escaut in 1966. There was particular scope for rationalisation in this case, since both firms were important producers of pipes and tubes, and their combined share of the total output of this category of product is over 80 per cent. As well as the mergers which formed the "front-rank" producers, other amalgamations involved several of the medium-sized producers.

The formation of the two leading groups has enabled the construction of new large-scale production facilities to be undertaken.[1] Usinor is developing a large

1 See 'Streamlining Steel Industry,' by Giles Merritt, *Financial Times,* 14 May 1973.

integrated coastal works at Dunquerque, which produced 3.3m. tons of crude steel in 1972, and which is scheduled to have an output of 4.5 m. tons in 1973, rising sharply to 8 m. tons in 1975. In 1969 Wendel Sidelor, facing the exhaustion of its iron ore deposits in Lorraine, began the construction of another major coastal complex at Fos-sur-Mer, near Marseilles, costing $1,800 m. at current prices, which is to have a designed capacity of 7 m. tons of crude steel by 1980. Wendel Sidelor has since been joined in this venture by Usinor, and by Thyssen of West Germany.

The structural changes indicate the efforts which the French industry has been making to improve its performance. It had the slowest annual rate of output growth – three per cent – of all the EEC countries between 1950 and 1969, and of all the countries of the enquiry, only the USA and the UK had worse growth rates (Table 1). It also had the worst profit performance of all the countries between 1962 and 1965, when post-tax profits as a proportion of total assets averaged 0.8 per cent.[1] This outcome can be attributed in part to the relatively slow growth of the French economy, in part to the fragmented structure of the industry before the major mergers, in part to strong competition in export markets, and in part also to Government price control which was at its most stringent in the mid-1960s.

However, while the Government has intervened on prices it has also given the industry considerable financial assistance for modernisation and rationalisation. To date there have been six four-year 'plans professionels'. The current one runs until 1975 and provides for investments totalling around $4,000m., or twice the level of the Fifth Plan. A substantial part of this is provided by the Government as low-interest loans. The plans have been important in aiding the rationalisation of the industry during a period of low profitability, and have assisted not only development by the major producers but also those by smaller manufacturers. One of the most important of the latter has been the construction of a scrap-based steel-works with electric arc furnaces at Isbergues by Châtillon-Commentry-Biache and Creusot-Loire.[2] This type of assistance with joint ventures helped the medium-sized producer to obtain additional economies of scale, but further entire mergers between them are clearly a distinct possibility in the future.

(c) Germany, F.R.[3]

Output in Western Germany grew at about the same rate as in the EEC as a whole in the post-war period (7 per cent). Profitability, at any rate during the first half of the 1960s, was low, with the ratio of post-tax profits to total assets registering 1.9 per cent in the period 1962 to 1965.[4]

This moderate growth and profit performance belies the basic strength of the industry. It is the largest producer of the countries of this enquiry after the US and Japan, and in 1969 had an output of 45 million tons of crude steel, equal to 42 per cent of the output of the entire European Community in that year. In 1963,

---

1   J. Singer, *Trade Liberalisation and the Canadian Steel Industry*, (Toronto: University of Toronto Press), 1969, Table 26, p. 51.

2   Chambre Syndicale de la Sidérurgie Française, op. cit., 1971, p. 67.

3   At the time of writing, no fieldwork in Germany has been conducted.

4   J. Singer, op. cit., 1969, Table 26, p. 51.

there were 61 enterprises classified to the iron and steel industry operating 92 works.[1] The average size of the larger plants (though not of the larger firms) is greater than for any of the other EEC countries (Table 16), and as Table 21 indicates, towards the end of the 1960s a higher proportion of total steelmaking capacity was contained in both plants and firms with capcities of 5 million tons and above than in the other Community countries (and the UK and Canada). Comparable data for the mid-1950s cannot be computed, so it is impossible to show the extent to which the large firms and plants have increased in importance.

The improvements in efficiency through structural developments have not kept pace with the demands of a growing and maturing economy. Wage inflation outstripped rises in productivity between 1960 and 1967 to yield an increase in labour costs per unit of crude steel output double that for the entire Community and second only to that for the Netherlands (Table 15). These rises have been reflected in prices and import penetration rose from an average 14 per cent of apparent consumption during the 1950s to 35 per cent in 1969 (Table 4).

Table 21 *Germany, F.R.: Distribution of Crude Steelmaking Capacity by Size of Firm and Plant, late 1960s*

Capacity Range (m. tons)	Percentage of Capacity	
	Firms	Plants
Below 0.5	2.3	4.6
0.5 – 0.9	4.0	10.6
1.0 – 1.9	26.3	30.1
2.0 – 4.9	5.4	39.9
5.0 and above	61.9	14.8
Total	100.0	100.0
Total capacity of estimates (m. tons)	44.8	44.8

Source: as for Table 18.

That there is considerable scope for further concentration and rationalisation at the level of the firm is indicated by Table 22. Eleven firms produced over a million tons of crude steel in 1969, and the output concentration ratio for the three largest firms was 51.4 per cent, lower than for any other country except the two major producers, the USA and Japan. The seven largest manufacturers provide a full range of steel products, while the others concentrate upon either flat or light or heavy rolled products. The slow pace of rationalisation can be attributed both to the low profitability of the industry in recent years and to the traditional conservatism of German steel producers.

Some attempt at obtaining benefits from specialisation began in 1967 when the common steel producers arranged themselves into four regional groups to allow the distribution of steel (and, to some degree, its production) to be better coordinated. This agreement was approved by the Commission of the EEC provided that the groups did not collaborate with each other.[2] Eventually the agreement led to a

1   Office Statistique des Communautés Européennes, *Résultats définitifs de l'Enquête Industrielle de 1963,*(Brussels), 1969, Tables A. 01 and D. 01.

2   *The Economist,* 22 November 1969, p. 86.

full merger proposal in 1968 between three members of the "Nord" syndicate, Klöckner, Salzgitter and Ilseder. One of the major benefits which, it was anticipated, would flow from this, was the coordination of investment activity, allowing both a reduction in the overall level of new capital expenditure and the construction of larger individual production facilities. But the proposal collapsed the following year due to objections by (unprofitable) Salzgitter and Ilseder over the dominance of (profitable) Klöckner. However, Thyssen and Mannesmann did set up a joint company to pool their steel tube interests.[1] The four syndicates were reorganized and expanded in 1971 to increase the degree of product specialisation by members. The object is to allow some companies to specialise in certain types of products, while others concentrate on particular qualities and dimensions.[2] While this will allow some increase in the degree of specialisation possible within the existing corporate framework of the German industry, it can be seen essentially as a temporary measure.

Table 22 *Germany, F.R.: Crude Steel Production by, and Shares in National Output of, Major Steel Companies, 1969*

Company	Crude Steel Production (m. tons)	Share in National Output (%)
Thyssen	12.23	27.0
Hoesch	6.66	14.7
Krupp	4.40	9.7
Mannesmann	3.40	7.5
Klöckner	3.38	7.5
Salzgitter	2.30	5.1
Röchlingsche	1.80	4.0
Ilseder	1.64	3.6
Dillingen	1.60	3.5
Neunkircher	1.20	2.6
Rheinische Stahlwerke	1.10	2.4
Total of 11 largest producers	39.71	87.6
Others	5.61	12.4
Total	45.32	100.0

Source: B.S.C. data

Extensive rationalisation and development at the levels of both firm and plant are necessary to assure the longer-term well-being of the German industry. There have already been some steps in this direction. Since 1970, Salzgitter has absorbed Ilseder, and Hoesch has merged with Hoogovens of the Netherlands. In 1973 Thyssen took over Rheinische Stahlwerke (although not without resistance from some of the latter's shareholders).[3] The Hoesch-Hoogovens link will enable a new

1   *The Economist,* 29 March 1969, p. 71.

2   'EEC Commission approves steel industry reshuffle in Germany' by Reginald Dale, *Financial Times,* 29 July 1971.

3   'Board rides out criticism of "expropriation" terms', by Andrew Hargrave, *Financial Times,* 16 August 1973.

large-scale coastal works to be built near Rotterdam, environmentalists permitting. After the initial post-war surge in investment in Germany, new plant construction has been very limited, the bulk of the funds being channelled into the expansion and modernisation of existing works. While most of these have access to deliveries of water-borne raw materials coming up the Rhine, and can ship out their final products by the same means, there has been a lack of tide-water sites, which the German-Dutch merger will overcome.

Plans have also been made by some of the major producers to develop mini-mills, and Klöckner has entered into an agreement with Korf, the owner of the relevant patents in West Germany.[1] An additional response by several of the major producers is to consolidate their positions by expanding their investments in metal-using industries.

(d) Italy[2]

The Italian steel industry produced 16 million tons of crude steel in 1969, or 15 per cent of the total output of the EEC. Since 1950 production has increased at an average annual rate of 13 per cent, twice as fast as the growth in the Community as a whole (Table 1). The rapid rate of expansion is attributable largely to the fast rate of development of the Italian economy in the post-war period.

The industry is very fragmented. In 1963 there were 398 enterprises classified to the general iron and steel category, operating 524 establishments, an enterprise-to-establishment ratio of 1.3.[3] Although Italy is only the fourth-largest of the five producing areas in the EEC, she possesses the greatest number of enterprises and establishments. The great bulk of these are, however, re-rolling and finishing units. *Iron and Steelworks of the World* lists only 26 steel-producing companies in production towards the end of the 1960s, operating 32 steel-producing plants.[4]

Table 23 details the three major producers in 1969. Italsider, which accounts for over half the total output, is part of the State-owned Finsider group, and received considerable investment finance from IRI, the State industrial development corporation. Fiat, the automobile manufacturer, is the third largest producer, and manufactures largely for its own use. Each of the major manufacturers produces a full range of flat, light and heavy rolled products; the remaining twenty or so companies concentrate mainly upon reinforcing bars. The range of the industry's output is continually expanding and its quality improving, but as Table 2 shows it is still characterised by a high proportion (35 per cent in 1969) of bars, rods and light sections, a higher ratio than for any other nation. Re-rolling units generally employ imported ingots and billets, and in 1968 these were the second-largest category of imports following only plate and sheet of less than 3mm. thickness.[5]

1 'The Changing Face of German Steel', by Frank Vogl, *The Times*, 23 February 1973.

2 Italy is another country which has not yet been included on our field-work itinerary. This is a pity, since published material on the industry appears to be scarce. The section presents such information as we have been able to glean so far.

3 Office Statistique des Communautés Européennes, op. cit., 1969.

4 H.G. and G. Cordero (eds.), op. cit., 1969.

5 British Steel Corporation, *Statistical Handbook 1968*, op. cit.

Table 23 *Italy: Crude Steel Production by, and Share in National Output of, Major Steel Companies, 1969*

Company	Crude Steel Production (million tons)	Share in National Output (%)
Italsider	9.44	57.5
Falck	1.14	6.9
Fiat	1.10[a]	6.7
Total of 3 largest producers	11.68	71.1
Others	4.74	28.9
Total	16.42	100.0

Notes: (a) estimated
Source: B.S.C. data.

In the period since the mid-1950s, the numbers of both firms and plants which make crude steel have declined slightly, and the average size of the larger units has increased. The upward shift in the size-distribution of firms and plants is clearly shown in Table 24. Whereas at the start of the period (*circa* 1956) there were no companies with capacities of 2 million tons, by the end of the 1960s the formation of Italsider had produced a company with a capacity of over 5 million tons, and which contributed more than one-half of total capacity. Large plants had similarly increased in importance, although there were, by the late-1960s, still no units of 5 millions tons capacity, and very small units with capacities of below 0.5 million tons accounted for about one-fifth of total capacity. The continued survival of the small unit reflects the importance of low grade light-rolled products, which can be produced from scrap in small plants.

The development of the large plant has been due largely to State aid to Italsider via the IRI to construct a major integrated works at Taranto in Southern Italy, designed to be expanded to an eventual capacity of 5 million tons. The site for this plant was chosen mainly with the depressed conditions of that part of Italy in mind, and a further similar development is planned.

In spite of its fast rate of growth, the annual increase in home demand for steel in Italy is insufficient to allow major large-scale integrated works to be built very frequently, and some nations, particularly the US, fear that a consequence of this may be an agressive exporting drive to expand production.[1] The possibility of the success of such a measure is aided by the low cost of labour in Italy (Table 14).

(e) The Netherlands

The steel industry in the Netherlands is the smallest and the fastest growing of the countries of the EEC: in 1969 just under 5 million tons of crude steel were produced, and the annual average rate of increase since 1950 was 22 per cent (Table 1). The expansion of the industry has resulted both from the growth of the Dutch economy and from the development of export markets. Exports as a proportion of production rose sharply from an annual average of 58 per cent during the 1950s to over 90 per cent at the end of the 1960s. At the same time, the proportion of

1 Committee on Finance, US Senate, op. cit., 1967, p. 204.

Table 24 *Italy: Distribution of Crude Steelmaking Capacity by Size of Firm and Plant, mid-1950s and late-1960s*

Capacity Range (m. tons)	Percentage of Capacity			
	Firms		Plants	
	mid-1950s	late-1960s	mid-1950s	late-1960s
Below 0.5	42.9	18.1	53.1	20.7
0.5 – 0.9	29.3	6.4	29.3	6.4
1.0 – 1.9	27.8	22.9	17.6	29.4
2.0 – 4.9	–	–	–	43.6
5.0 and above	–	52.6	–	–
Total	100.0	100.0	100.0	100.0
Total capacity of estimates (m. tons)	6.9	17.7	6.9	17.7

Source: as for Table 18.

domestic consumption satisfied by imports has remained very high, at around 90 per cent (Table 4). The importance of both exports and imports occurs chiefly because of the substantial amounts of semi-finished products which are exported for re-rolling and finishing and then re-imported.

During the entire post-war period the Dutch industry has comprised of three steelmaking firms — Ablesserdam, Demka and Hoogovens — each operating a single plant. Hoogovens is the only integrated unit producing steel by the BOS route, and has an estimated annual crude steel capacity of 3.1 million tons, equal to 89 per cent of the industry's capacity. It manufactures a range of flat, light and heavy rolled products. In 1971, it merged with Hoesch of Germany to construct a new coastal works near Rotterdam (see (c) above). Of the remaining two companies Demka is very small with a capacity of 47,000 tons and produces wire and light castings, and Ablesserdam has a crude steel capacity of 350,000 tons and manufactures rods, strip and wire.

The Netherlands steel industry (which virtually equals Hoogovens) is generally recognised as one of the most efficient in the world. During the first part of the 1960s it registered an average annual rate of post-tax profit on total assets of 5.6 per cent, second only to the outcome for Canada (and ranked first on the basis of post-tax profits to revenue).[1] Labour productivity is also very high (Table 14).

(f) The European Economic Community

A brief note is appropriate at this point referring to the effect of the EEC customs union upon trade by and between the steel industries of the member countries, and to the role of the Commission in fostering increased efficiency while endeavouring to promote competition.

The European Coal and Steel Community was established in 1952, and tariffs between the members were removed on 1 May 1953.[2] The ECSC merged with

1 J. Singer, op. cit., Table 26, p. 51.

2 D. Burn, *The Steel Industry, 1939–1959,* (Cambridge: Cambridge University Press), 1961 pp. 389, 416.

the EEC in 1968. Since the establishment of the ECSC trade in steel by the member countries has expanded substantially. To consider recent experience, between 1960 and 1968, the combined volume of exports rose by 55 per cent (from 23 to 36 million tons), and the share of intra-community trade rose from 42 to 48 per cent.[1]

Without detailed analysis it is of course impossible to indicate the contribution of tariff removal to these developments. Conventionally, customs unions are thought to promote trade between members by encouraging countries and industries to specialise upon those products or activities in which they have net comparative advantage (trade creation) and, by establishing a common external tariff wall, to remove the comparative advantage of some third-country producers (trade diversion). There is very little evidence of a marked increase in specialisation among the EEC steel industries. During the 1960s the overall composition of the total final output of the several industries changed very little. Flat-rolled products tended to increase slightly in importance in Belgium-Luxembourg, Germany, F.R. and Italy, while semi-manufactures and bars developed in the Netherlands. There were scarcely any changes in France. These trends were also closely reflected in the development of exports.[3] Where the customs union is likely to have had its greatest impact upon the steel industries, therefore, is in encouraging a faster rate of growth than would otherwise have occurred, allowing larger firms and plants to develop. Just how much the formation of the EEC has contributed to faster growth remains a moot point at this stage.

The High Authority of the ECSC has offered encouragement to each steel industry to raise its efficiency. In a study of the likely developments in the European steel industry during the latter part of the 1960s, the High Authority defined four major requirements. The need to increase the scale of individual steel-works was seen as a prime necessity. The high cost of ECSC iron ore and coal, relative to imported supplies, was also seen as a considerable problem and efforts were required to improve the efficiency of supply and to remove intra-community differences in costs. Closer collaboration between steel users and producers was urged to allow the variety of types and dimensions of steel products to be reduced, and to aid producers to develop new products and explore new uses for steel. Finally, the High Authority recognised that improvements in efficiency must accord with the social and regional policies of the Community. The High Authority was prepared to assist these developments, and was prepared to allow increases in concentration through mergers.[4] A consequence of this policy was a loan from the European Bank for Investment for Italsider's new steelworks at Taranto. By 1971, it was reported that the ECSC had plans to allow the 30 major producers of the Community to merge into 10 groups, each with a maximum permitted output of about 20 million

1 British Steel Corporation, *Statistical Handbooks, 1960 and 1968,* op. cit.

2 cf. J. Viner, *The Customs Union Issue,* (New York: Carnegie), 1950.

3 British Steel Corporation, *Statistical Handbooks 1960–8,* op. cit.

4 Haute Autorité, *Objectifs Généraux Acier, Memorandum sur les objectifs de 1970,* (Luxembourg: Communauté Européenne du Charbon et de l'Acier), pp. 114–6.

tons, or 12–13 per cent of total EEC production.[1] Certainly, this is the kind of development to be expected if the Community is to reap the benefits of economic integration on a scale comparable to that of the USA.

(g) The United Kingdom

The steel industry in the UK is dominated by the British Steel Corporation (BSC) which in 1969 accounted for 91 per cent (24.6 million tons) of all domestically produced crude steel and in terms of the value of both sales and assets was the second largest steel company in the world, following only U.S. Steel Corporation.[2] The BSC was formed in 1967 to take over the assets of the 14 largest crude steel producing companies which passed into public ownership under the steel national-isation act of the same year.[3] Companies with individual crude steel outputs of less than 482,600 tons remained in the private sector. The companies whose assets were absorbed are detailed in Table 25, together with an indication of their finished steel output levels. In 1964–5 the four largest producers accounted for 54 per cent of the total deliveries of finished products from UK manufacturers.

Table 25 *United Kingdom: Production of Finished Steel by Companies absorbed by the British Steel Corporation, 1964–5 (or 1963–4)*

Company	Production of Finished Steel '000 tons
United Steel Co.	3438
Richard Thomas and Baldwins	3350
Steel Company of Wales	2780
Colvilles	2700
Stewarts and Lloyds	2032
Dorman, Long & Co.	1972
G.K.N. Steel Co.	1920[b]
John Summers	1702
South Durham Steel and Iron Co.	1497
Consett Iron Co.	1008
Tube Investment (Park Gate Iron and Steel Co. and Round Oak Steel Works[a])	994[b]
Lancashire Steel Corp.	669
English Steel Corp.	513[b]

Source: *The Economist,* 30 July 1966, p. 454.
Notes: (a) Round Oak Steel Works was subsequently returned to the private sector.
(b) 1963–4 figures.

Although the BSC accounts for virtually all the output of crude steel, its share of the UK market for finished products varies considerably. In 1968–9 its market share[4] ranged from over 80 per cent for such products as rails, heavy sections and

1 'How the B.S.C. will be shackled if Britain joins the E.E.C.', by Kennedy Lindsay, *The Guardian,* 9 June 1971, p. 22. This was the notorious article in which Professor Lindsay claimed the E.C.S.C. intended to stop any further expansion of the B.S.C.

2 British Steel Corporation, *Annual Report and Accounts, 1968–69,* (London), 1970, p. 36.

3 *Iron and Steel Act, 1967,* (London: H.M.S.O.), 1967.

4 Net domestic deliveries plus imports.

bars, sheet, plate and tinplate, through 50 to 80 per cent for semi-manufactures, wheels, tubes, wire and hot-rolled strip, etc., and 10 to 50 per cent for hot-rolled bars, light sections and cold-rolled strip, etc., to 8 per cent each for castings and special steels.[1]

In addition to the BSC there are over 130 independent companies in the iron and steel industry, including approximately 11 iron-making, 34 steel-making, and 86 rolling and finishing concerns.[2] The pig iron producers supply almost exclusively foundries, the steel makers produce predominantly special grades, while the rolling and finishing enterprises are concerned chiefly with the re-rolling of semi-manufactures, using either domestic or imported materials. The latter continue to exist largely through their ability to handle small orders for particular qualities or sizes of products.

The BSC is fairly heavily integrated forward into steel-using operations, and is also diversified into activities connected with the main business of steel-making. In 1969, wire-making, plant and machine tool manufacture, structural and pipework engineering, and other steel-using activities, together with stockholding and merchanting contributed 6.7 per cent of gross turnover, while a further 0.6 per cent was provided by ancillary activities including brickmaking and the production of concrete pipes.[3]

The steel industry is not, however, so concerned with the stockholding and distribution of finished products as is generally the case elsewhere. Independent stockholders and merchants account for the largest single share of deliveries to various classes of consumers, and absorbed about one-quarter of the total in 1969,[4] a proportion which has tended to increase in recent years. This system, which reduces contact between the steel producer and the final customer has been accused of amplifying the cyclical variations in demand at the production stage.[5]

Throughout the entire post-war period the steel industry has been the subject of severe political debate and control. It was first nationalised by the Labour Government in 1950, but in the following year a Conservative administration enacted legislation largely returning it to private ownership. This was in the main achieved by 1955, although Richard Thomas and Baldwins was retained, largely because its unprofitable condition precluded its sale. Until renationalisation in 1967, the number of firms and plants in the industry remained fairly constant. The Census of Production for 1958 showed that there were 330 enterprises operating 512 establishments in the Iron and Steel (General) category of the UK Standard Industrial Classification, which includes iron-making, and rolling and finishing in addition to steelmaking.[6]

1 British Steel Corporation, op. cit., 1970.

2 According to H.G. and G. Cordero (eds.), op. cit., 1969. J. Singer, op. cit., 1969, p. 78, indicates that there were 210 companies left in the private sector.

3 British Steel Corporation, op. cit., 1970.

4 British Steel Corporation, *Statistical Handbook 1969,* op. cit.

5 Christopher Blake, op. cit., 1965.

6 Board of Trade, *Report on the Census of Production for 1958,* (London: H.M.S.O.)

In 1963 the comparable figures were 341 and 544 respectively, indicating an average 1.6 establishments per enterprise.[1] Although the number of units remained fairly static until 1966,[2] the average sizes of both firms and plants tended to increase, but at a slower rate than elsewhere (see Table 16).

The increase in the firm and plant average capacities were accompanied by an upward movement in the size-distributions, as Table 26 shows. For the reasons given in Appendix 4, the percentage values shown in the table should be treated with caution: the total crude steelmaking capacities obtained over-estimate the size of the industry in the late-1960s and substantially underestimate it for the earlier analysis. In addition, the method used provides a bias towards larger plants and firms in the late-1960s analysis and the reverse for the mid-1950s study. Despite these qualifications, however, we are confident that the table broadly summarises the situation satisfactorily. By the late-1960s, three-quarters of total crude steel output was in firms with capacities of 2 million tons or above, while the corresponding ratio for plants was 31 per cent. The developments were achieved through scrapping small, obsolete facilities, and modernising and expanding the larger plants.

However, these improvements did not keep pace with developments in the other major steel industries, and productivity rose slower, and costs faster, than abroad. The rate of return on capital employed by the 14 major companies fell from 15 per cent in 1956 to 6.1 per cent in 1965, with a low of 4.3 per cent in 1963.[3] Investment varied with the steel cycle, rising during the later part of the 1950s and the first two years of the 1960s, but falling sharply from $476 million in 1962 to $117 million in 1966. Particularly in the later years, investment per ton of crude steel output was very low in comparison with the rates achieved elsewhere (see Table 5).

This sluggish performance can be attributed to three main factors:

(i) *Price Control:* During the post-war period of private ownership, maximum prices were set by the Iron and Steel Board for most categories of steel products. A consequence of this was that producers were unable to raise their prices above the maximum in boom periods, and their profitability suffered as a result. Until the judgement on the Heavy Steel Makers' Agreement in the Restrictive Practices Court in 1964,[4] the maximum prices also served as minima in the producers' lists, but secret price cutting was prevalent in depressed periods.[5] Hence, low or even negative profitability in the slump could not be offset by high profits in the boom.

(ii) *Surplus Capacity:* Even allowing for cyclical variations in demand, there was a trend increase in the percentage of unused capacity in the industry throughout the

1 Board of Trade, *Report on the Census of Production for 1963*, (London: H.M.S.O.)

2 There were one or two mergers between the major producers immediately prior to nationalisation.

3 Development Coordinating Committee, *The Steel Industry, Stage I Report*, (London: British Iron and Steel Federation), 1966, Appendix 17, pp. 134–5.

4 LR 5 RP 33, summarised in Registrar of Restrictive Trading Agreements, op. cit., 1966, pp. 22–4.

5 C.K. Rowley, op. cit., 1971, pp. 89–90.

Table 26 *United Kingdom: Distribution of Crude Steelmaking Capacity by Size of Firm and Plant, mid-1950s and late-1960s*

Capacity Range (m. tons)	Percentage of Capacity			
	Firms		Plants	
	mid-1950s	late-1960s	mid-1950s	late-1960s
Below 0.5	20.2	7.1	31.7	15.2
0.5 – 0.9	8.1	5.0	23.6	26.7
1.0 – 1.9	38.7	12.7	31.0	27.4
2.0 – 4.9	33.0	60.7	13.5	30.7
5.0 and above	–	14.5	–	–
Total	100.0	100.0	100.0	100.0
Total Capacity of Estimates (m. tons)	15.0	38.1	15.0	38.1

Source: as for Table 18.

period. In 1955 the degree of utilisation was 98 per cent; by 1966 it had fallen to 78.8 per cent. This occurred largely as a result of the failure of the forecast increase in demand for steel products to materialise, and unit costs were elevated as a consequence. In addition, the development of chronic surplus capacity was a feature of the steel industries of most other countries, and this depressed export prices.

(iii) *Government Intervention:* For regional and social reasons the Government on several occasions directed both the timing and the location of new plant construction Probably the most famous case was Prime Minister Macmillan's self-styled "judgement of Solomon" in 1958. Faced with a choice *between* two strip mills (proposed respectively by Richard Thomas and Baldwins of South Wales and Colvilles of Scotland) the Government succeeded in reducing the initial capacity of one and having *both* constructed, meeting the companies' investment shortfall itself. This resulted in the simultaneous provision of two sub-optimal facilities, neither of which could operate at full capacity and one at least of which was badly located.[1]

(iv) *Allocative Inefficiency:* Certain quarters, and in particular the nationalisation lobby, claimed that in an industry which was small-scale as compared with those of the US and Japan, the fragmentation of output over 14 companies meant that investment plans could not be coordinated sufficiently to ensure the replacement of existing plant with new facilities of optimal scale sufficiently swiftly.[2] Countering this argument, the steel producers claimed that product specialisation between them overcame much of the fragmentation accusation, and the industry-sponsored Benson report of 1966 was confident that extensive rationalisation and modernisation could be carried out leaving the corporate structure of the industry unchanged.[3]

1 Macmillan's biblical reference was ironically appropriate: cf. D. Burn, op. cit., 1961, p. 645, "...Solomon acted with a full understanding that if his judgement were carried out it would kill the child".

2 *Steel Nationalisation,* (London: H.M.S.O.), 1965.

3 Development Coordinating Committee, op. cit., 1966, esp. Chap. VII, pp. 77–85.

It was against this background of charge and countercharge that the majority of the industry passed into public ownership in 1967. Initially the BSC was organised on a regional basis, comprising largely, although not entirely, groupings of the previous companies. In 1970, however, the operating structure was reorganized on a product basis, with four steelmaking divisions covering general steels, special steels, strip mills and tubes, together with constructional engineering and chemicals. This development was designed to aid further the rationalisation process which had commenced after nationalisation. In its initial stages this has consisted primarily of the concentration of bulk steelmaking on the larger plants, the more efficient scheduling of production between plants, allowing higher degrees of product specialisation, and an extensive revision of sales and marketing operations. One effect of the latter has been the consolidation of the diverse overseas distribution network which the BSC inherited from the fragmented private-sector companies.

But in the longer term much more extensive rationalisation and modernisation plans are necessary to raise the efficiency of the industry and its international competitiveness. At the end of 1972 the BSC announced a ten-year development plan[1] and this was broadly confirmed by the Government in a White Paper published in February of the following year.[2] The plan calls for an investment expenditure of $7.2 billion to expand the BSCs crude steelmaking capacity from its present level of 27 million tons to 33—35 million tons by the late 1970s and to 36—38 million tons during the first half of the 1980s. The bulk of this output will come from five centres using the BOS route: Port Talbot and Llanwern in Wales, Ravenscraig in Scotland, Scunthorpe and Teesside in England. The largest of these will be Teesside with an eventual total annual capacity of about 12 million tons, with Ravenscraig the smallest with an output of about 3.2 million tons a year. Each of the centres currently makes steel, and the existing facilities are to be modernised and expanded. In addition a new works was brought on stream at Scunthorpe in 1973[3] and a plant with an eventual capacity of 7 million tons annually is planned for Teesside to supplement the Lackenby works. Additional supplies, especially of high-grade carbon and special steels, will come from small-scale electric arc plants in the Sheffield area and elsewhere. Several small, obsolete plants are to be closed, and the BSC expects to shed 30,000 jobs by the end of the period.

The BSC is thus entering on a lengthy period of heavy investment, the full benefits of which will not be felt until the middle of the next decade. In the three years following nationalisation, it succeeded in raising investment per ton of annual output from $7.5 to $13.7,[4] but coupled with severe restrictions on prices, this has caused low profitability to deteriorate steadily, and losses totalled $312 million in 1971—72.[5] The limitations on prices have derived both from pressure on export

1 See 'Steel: turning a heritage into a humdinger', by Roger Eglin, *Sunday Times,* 24 December 1972, p. 17.

2 Department of Trade and Industry, *Steel,* (London: HMSO) Cmnd. 5226, 1973.

3 'Anchor Project', *The Times,* 12 February 1973.

4 British Steel Corporation, *Annual Report and Accounts 1970—71,* (London: HMSO), 1972.

5 British Steel Corporation, *Annual Report and Accounts 1971—72,* (London: HMSO), 1973.

prices during periods of low demand, and, since the ending of regulation by the Iron and Steel Board, Government intervention on home prices. Proposed price rises averaging about 7 per cent were (for a time) cut to just above 5 per cent on the advice of the National Board for Prices and Incomes in 1969 on the grounds that greater efforts to contain costs could be made.[1] In 1971 the new Conservative adminstration cut by half the BSC's proposals for a 14 per cent average increase.[2] With Britain's entry into the European Economic Community on 1 January 1973 the Government lost the *de jure* power to influence steel prices, but under the current counter-inflation strategy, the Prime Minister has stressed that the nationalised sector is to be in the van of price restraint.

In addition to the BSC's development programme, a private-sector company has constructed a semi-integrated steelworks using electric arc technology at Sheerness in the Greater London region with an initial annual capacity of 180,000 tons,[3] and a similar facility is planned (by a different concern) for the Manchester area.[4] Hence the UK industry is following, to some degree, the mini-mill trend of the United States, which industry we consider next.

(h) The United States
The USA is the largest steel producing country in the World, having an output of 128 million tons of crude steel in 1969. *Iron and Steelworks of the World*[5] lists for that period 224 companies in the iron and steel industry, of which 20 (9 per cent) were integrated steel producers, 74 (33 per cent) were non-integrated producers and the remaining 130 were variously concerned with iron-making, re-rolling and finishing.

Table 27 shows the crude steel production and share in national output of the major companies in 1969. U.S. Steel Corp., at that time the world's largest steel company, produced one-quarter of total industry output, and the four largest companies together accounted for over one-half. During the second half of the 1960s, the major producers generally maintained their output shares at a time when total output was expanding slowly, at around 2.5 per cent annually. The exception was Bethlehem Steel Corp., the second-largest producer which suffered a reduction in output share of almost one percentage point between 1967 and 1969. Among the other, smaller, companies which together account for about one-fifth of total output,

1 National Board for Prices and Incomes, *Steel Prices*, Cmnd. 4033, (London: HMSO), 1969, esp. paras. 38 and 84. The Board also recommended that the permitted average increase should not be obtained, wholly or partly, through raising prices on products in which the BSC had a dominant market share, or for which increases had been claimed which would raise rates of return (on fixed and current assets) above the targets (para. 86), and that some modification should be made to the proposed revision of the structure of extras and allowances (para. 88).

2 *Economist*, 10 April 1971, p. 74.

3 'A new steelworks on London's doorstep' by Ken Gofton, *Financial Times*, 10 November 1972.

4 'The mini-mill concept comes to Britain', by Ken Gofton, *Financial Times*, 10 November 1972.

5 H.G. and G. Cordero (eds.) op. cit., 1969.

the tendency has been for the very small producers to decline at the expense of their larger competitors.

Table 27 *United States: Crude Steel Production by and Share in National Output of, Major Steel Companies, 1969*

Company	Crude Steel Production (million tons)	Share in National Output (%)
U.S. Steel Corp.	31.50	24.6
Bethlehem Steel Corp.	19.75	15.4
Republic Steel Corp.	9.75	7.6
National Steel Corp.	8.03	6.3
Armco	7.44	5.8
Jones and Laughlin	7.05	5.5
Inland Steel Corp.	6.80	5.3
Youngstown Sheet and Tube	5.46	4.3
Wheeling-Pittsburgh Steel Corp.	3.64	2.8
Kaiser Steel Corp.	2.69	2.1
Ford Motor Co.	2.50[a]	2.0
Total of 11 largest	104.61	81.7
Others	23.36	18.3
Total	127.97	100.0

Source: B.S.C. data
Notes: (a) estimated

By comparison with the other countries of this enquiry, the degree of product specialisation at both company and plant levels appears to be higher than elsewhere. In the late-1960s, almost 20 per cent of the crude steel capacity in companies of 2 million tons capacity and above was in units which produced flat-rolled products only, whereas in every other country companies in this size-group invariably produced a full range of flat, heavy and light-rolled products. Similarly, the proportions of capacity in companies of smaller scales with relatively narrow product ranges is generally higher than elsewhere.[1] In addition, since average plant and firm sizes in the US are greater than elsewhere (Table 16), there is scope for companies manufacturing a diversity of steel products to obtain production runs of above-average length and (so far as transport costs allow) to concentrate the production of particular products on particular plants. Similar benefits are present when special steel manufacture is considered: Allegheny-Ludlum is the major specialist producer, having at the end of the 1960s a capacity of 2.5 million tons and ranking 14th in the industry on this basis.[2]

Of the three major steel producers, U.S. Steel Corp. has developed forward integration and diversification to the greatest extent, having steel-using divisions which include constructional engineering (particularly bridges), oilwell plant and machinery, containers and pre-engineered housing, together with chemicals, plastics and cement divisions. Bethlehem's major steel-using division is shipbuilding, while

1   Estimated from H.G. and G. Cordero (eds.) op. cit., 1969.

2   Ibid.

Republic, at the time of our interviews, had not integrated very much. Among the medium-sized producers, Jones and Laughlin was acquired by the conglomerate LTV in 1967,[1] and Ford Motor Co. is a substantial sheet steel producer for its own use.

Stockholding is an important function for most US steel producers, and about 80 per cent of domestic sales are made direct to the consumer. Manufacturers see this as an essential requirement for providing a speedy and efficient service and for obtaining information on the state of demand. It is also a valuable means of building consumer loyalty for a product which in each category it is difficult for producers to differentiate. Independent distributors who supply a full range of general steel products draw their stocks from several producers, although those which concentrate on special steels frequently develop close ties with particular manufacturers.

In the post-war period, there has been a slight tendency for the number of iron and steel companies to increase, while the number of plants in operation has tended to decline. In 1958 there were 148 companies operating 291 establishments in industry 3312 of the U.S. Standard Industrial Classification (Blast Furnaces and Steel Mills) and by 1963, the corresponding figures were 161 and 288, a plant-to-company ratio of 1.8.[2] These trends occured through rationalisation among the medium and large size producers, exits by some small manufacturers, and the establishment of new, small-scale, scrap-based facilities.

Table 28 *United States: Distribution of Crude Steelmaking Capacity by Size of Firm and Plant, mid-1950s and late-1960s*

Capacity Range (m. tons)	Percentage of Capacity			
	Firms		Plants	
	mid-1950s	late-1960s	mid-1950s	late-1960s
Below 0.5	6.4	3.4	9.8	4.6
0.5 – 0.9	5.6	2.4	11.8	4.3
1.0 – 1.9	8.8	8.3	32.8	13.1
2.0 – 2.9	23.9	11.8	35.3	41.5
5.0 and above	55.2	74.2	10.4	36.5
Total	100.0	100.0	100.0	100.0
Total Capacity of Estimates (m. tons)	112.8	213.4	112.8	213.4

Source: as for Table 18.

As early as the mid-1950s, firms and plants with capacities of 5 million tons or above were significant features of the US industry as Table 28 shows, and their

1 Following Justice Department activity, LTV was forced to divest itself of several subsidiaries in order to retain the steel company.

2 Department of Commerce, Bureau of the Census, *1963 Census of Manufactures,* Vol. 2, part 2, (Washington, D.C.: U.S. Government Printing Office), 1966, Section 33A–7, Table 1.

importance increased substantially during the ensuing decade and a half. The development of the larger firms during the post-war period resulted primarily from internal growth through the construction of new plants and the modernisation and expansion of existing ones, rather than through merger. The rate of investment per ton of crude steel output increased firmly through the 1960s (Table 5) and despite depressed trading conditions in the later years was relatively high in comparison with the other countries. A few new steelmaking facilities — among them Bethlehem's Burn's Harbor, Indiana, complex — were constructed. The chief reason for this internal growth has been the continuing threat of antitrust action by the Justice Department, which was given material reinforcement in 1968 through the publication of the circumstances under which acquisitions would normally be challenged.[1] A few mergers among and between medium and small producers have taken place without challenge — for example that between Wheeling and Pittsburgh in 1968 — but the structural impact has been negligible.

As elsewhere, and as reflected in Table 28, the companies which have encountered the severest trading difficulties have been medium-sized enterprises with a wide product range of general steels. Until recently, small concerns producing special alloy steels, have generally maintained their market representation. One such firm which we interviewed overcame the large minimum scale requirement imposed at the primary rolling (ingot-to-billet) stage by contracting-out this work to nearby general steel producers, and then taking back the product for further rolling and processing. While this is not, apparently, typical, it illustrates one way in which scale disadvantages can be reduced. A major recent development which has slowed down the rate at which large plants have increased their importance in the industry has been the introduction of small-scale, semi-integrated plants employing electric arc furnaces and using locally generated scrap. These "mini-mills" have been constructed both by existing steel firms and by new entrants into the industry, and produce in the main common grades of rods and bars, often for reinforcing purposes, which are sold locally. The economic viability of these plants results from their ability to manufacture a narrow range of relatively low grade products, often using second-hand rolling mills, and, through their location close to both the sources of scrap and the final consumer, to reduce transport costs. However, their costs are extremely sensitive to the price of scrap, and when after 1968 scrap became scarcer, several went out of business.

In recent years the US steel industry has suffered declining profitability. Expressed in terms of the rate of return on total revenue, the ratio fell from a high of 6.1 per cent in the boom year of 1964 to 4.3 per cent in 1969, averaging 5.4 per cent annually during the period.[2] While some part of this is due to the cyclical reduction in the level of economic activity in the US during the later part of the period, some, and perhaps most of the decline reflects a trend fall in profitability. Although labour cost increases have been offset by rising productivity (Table 15), increases in raw material prices and capital expenditure have caused total unit costs to inflate, and this has not been recouped by equivalent increases in the prices of

1 Commerce Clearing House, Inc., *Merger Guidelines*, (New York), 1968.

2 American Iron and Steel Institute, *Annual Statistical Report, 1969*, (Washington, D.C.), 1970, Table 2.

final products. In part, the ability to raise prices has been limited by Presidential intervention (in 1962 and 1968), and partly also by the increasing penetration of imports, particularly from Japan.

Between 1960 and 1964, total imports formed slightly less than 5 per cent of apparent domestic consumption, but the ratio was 15 per cent by 1968, and 12 per cent in the following year (Table 4). Imports from Japan were 1.6 per cent of apparent consumption in 1964, but had risen to 4.8 per cent (or 32 per cent of all imports) by 1968.[1] The Senate staff study of 1967 attributed the increase in import penetration to generally lower factor costs (and particularly labour expenses) abroad, the development of excess capacity in the other major steel industries leading to intense competition (and accusations of dumping) in export markets, and also Government subsidies to foreign producers.[2] The American Iron and Steel Institute calculated that in 1965, neglecting transport costs, largely as a result of lower unit labour and capital charges, Japan could undersell the US industry by about 29 per cent, while the EEC producers taken together had an advantage of about 23 per cent.[3] The Senate enquiry recommended direct quantity controls as a short-term measure to alleviate the import problem, with multi-lateral discussions between producer nations to eliminate both the steel surplus and excessive price discrimination in export markets. It did not, perhaps, adequately recognise that the foreign producer ability to undersell the US industry in its own market resulted more from their natural cost advantages than from "unfair" trading practices.[4]

(i) Canada

Canada was one of the countries which we were unable to visit during the course of our enquiries, and the following review is drawn largely from Jacques Singer's comprehensive analysis of the international competitiveness of the Canadian steel industry.[5]

In the post-war period, the Canadian industry has achieved a relatively high rate of output growth, averaging 8 per cent annually between 1950 and 1969 (Table 1). Although still a net importer of steel products, the ratio of imports to apparent consumption fell from an annual average of 32 per cent between 1950 and 1959 to 20 per cent between 1966 and 1969 (Table 4). Singer attributes the growth of the industry to the general expansion of the economy, to the development of the Canadian consumer durables industries and to the expansion of steelmaking capacity allowing direct import substitution.

---

1   British Steel Corporation, *Statistical Handbook, 1965, 1968,* (London), 1966, 1969.

2   Committee on Finance U.S. Senate op. cit., 1967, esp. pp. XXIV–XXV.

3   American Iron and Steel Institute, *The Steel Import Problem,* (New York), 1968, Table G, p. 23.

4   Pricing imports below the level of domestically-manufactured goods is, of course, no evidence of dumping. What matters is the ratio of the import price to the producer's price in his home market.

5   J. Singer, op. cit., 1969.

6   Ibid., p. 12.

Iron and Steelworks of the World for the late-1960s lists 50 firms in the iron and steel industry, of which 17 have steelmaking facilities and the remainder are non-integrated pig iron producers or re-rollers and finishers.[1] Stelco, the largest steel-making firm, operates two plants, whilst the remaining producers operate a single facility each. Three firms account for about three-quarters of total crude steel output, as Table 29 shows. Between 1967 and 1969 the market shares of both Stelco and Algoma declined, and Dofasco replaced Algoma as the second largest crude steel producer. At the same time, the combined share of the smaller manufacturers increased from 17 to 24 per cent. Four companies — the three majors together with Dosco — are integrated producers of pig iron, crude steel and a range of rolling mill products, and are located in the eastern portion of the country. The remaining producers operate relatively small, scrap-based, plants west of the Great Lakes. Two of the three largest producers, Stelco and Algoma, produce fairly full ranges of rolling mill products, while Dofasco has concentrated on flat-rolled products, especially cold-rolled strip and sheet and tin-plate.

In the period since the mid-1950s the number of steel producers has risen from 10 to 17, and the average size of the larger firms has doubled (Table 16), the greater part of this increase resulting from the expansion of the plants of the major producers. Table 30 illustrates the redistribution of capacity, and emphasises the recent bi-polarisation between the major integrated producers and the small western firms producing steel from scrap in electric furnaces, several of whom are recent entrants to the industry. There have been no mergers involving the larger steel firms, as a result chiefly of the threat of anti-trust action.

Table 29 *Canada: Crude Steel Production by, and Share in National Output of, Major Steel Companies, 1969*

Company	Crude Steel Production (million tons)	Share in National Output (%)
Steel Company of Canada (Stelco)	3.33	36.2
Dominion Foundries and Steel (Dofasco)	2.07	22.4
Algoma Steel Corp.	1.57	17.0
Total of 3 largest producers	6.97	75.6
Others	2.24	24.4
Total	9.21	100.0

Source: B.S.C. data

The recent financial performance of the industry has also been good, as compared with that of the other nations. Between 1962 and 1965, profits after taxes were 7.2 per cent of total assets, yielding the highest ratio among the countries of our enquiry. The Canadian industry also ranked first when post-tax profits were expressed as a percentage of total shareholders' equity, and second (to the Netherlands)

1 H.G. and G. Cordero (eds.), op. cit., 1969.

Table 30. *Canada: Distribution of Crude Steelmaking Capacity by Size of Firm and Plant, mid-1950s and late-1960s*

Capacity Range (m. tons)	Percentage of Capacity Firms and Plants[a]	
	mid-1950s	late-1960s
Below 0.5	19.2	12.0
0.5 – 0.9	15.3	12.9
1.0 – 1.9	65.5	–
2.0 – 4.9	–	75.2
5.0 and above	–	–
Total	100.0	100.0
Total capacity of estimates (m. tons)	4.3	11.5

Notes: (a) All firms operate single plants.
Source: As for Table 18.

when they were calculated as a proportion of total revenue.[1]

Singer also analyses the international price competitiveness of the Canadian industry. He finds that lower ex-works prices, tariffs and the structure of freight rates serve to make the majority of Canadian steel products competitive vis-à-vis comparable products which could be imported from the US.[2] However, the recent declines in the export prices of the EEC producers and Japan "have widened the difference between offshore export prices and Canadian prices to theoretically permit flows of ECSC steel to eastern Canadian markets and Japanese steel into Vancouver".[3]

(j) Japan[4]

At the beginning of the post-war period the Japanese steel industry was virtually at a standstill, due primarily to extreme shortages of raw materials, and less importantly to war damage.[5] Since then the industry has achieved the fastest rate of growth of all the countries of the enquiry. It produced 4 million tons of crude steel in 1950, 22 million tons in 1960 and 82 million tons in 1968, an average annual rate of increase of 34 per cent (Table 1). Exports have played a significant role in this expansion, increasing their share of total production from an annual average of 16 per cent in the period 1950–1959, to 25 per cent in 1969 (Table 4). At the same time there have been stringent controls limiting imports.

There are more than 130 steelmaking firms, but only ten of these are fully

1 J. Singer, op. cit., 1969, Table 26, p. 51.

2 Ibid, Table 22, p. 45.

3 Ibid., p. 105.

4 As with Canada, the material for this case study has been obtained almost entirely from secondary sources, since no visit was possible. A valuable review of the development and present structure of the industry is in Kiyoshi Kawahito, *The Japanese Steel Industry,* (New York: Praeger), 1972, which also contains a study of the determinants of US steel imports from Japan.

5 Ibid., pp. 3–5.

integrated companies. The latter account for over 90 per cent of total steelmaking capacity and in 1969 the seven largest accounted for two-thirds of total crude steel output. The sizes of the largest plants and firms are 93 per cent and 66 per cent respectively of those in the US, but the individual major items of equipment are generally larger and more modern. For example, in 1968 the Japanese industry had seven of the world's largest ten blast furnaces[1] and most of its strip mills were installed after 1960, in contrast to the US where most of this type of equipment was installed prior to 1955.[2] In addition, Japan produces a markedly higher proportion of crude steel output via the BOS route than any other country (Table 7). This is reflected in the high proportion of pig-iron to scrap which is used (65 to 35 per cent in 1968). All iron ore is imported, since Japan has no indigenous resources, and a large part of the scrap requirement is also obtained abroad, much of it from the US. The larger steelworks are located at tidewater sites and this aids both the receipt of imported raw materials and the exportation of finished products.

Table 31 *Japan: Crude Steel Production by, and Share in National Output of, Major Steel Companies, 1969.*

Company	Crude Steel Production (million tons)	Share in National Output (%)
Yawata	15.28	18.6
Fuji	13.81	16.8
Nippon K.K.	11.41	13.6
Sumitomo	9.89	12.0
Kawasaki	10.06	12.3
Kobe	4.00	4.9
Nisshin	2.50	3.0
Total of 7 largest producers	66.68	81.2
Others	15.47	18.8
Total	82.15	100.0

Source: B.S.C. data.

However, while the vast bulk of output is produced by large scale organisations, the remainder is accounted for by fragmented and outdated facilities. There are between 400 and 550 re-rollers.[3] The existence of two such sectors is typical of many Japanese industries and is referred to as the 'dual structure'. With respect to the steel industry, small units continue to exist by fulfilling small orders for low-quality products, through cost reductions by operating at night when electricity is cheap, by paying low wages, and by avoiding many overheads necessarily incurred in large facilities. In addition they are protected by the *Keiretsu* system, under which larger firms provide technical and financial assistance in return for the use of their production facilities.

1 Ibid., p. 53.

2 Ibid., p. 50.

3 Ibid., p. 59.

Table 31 lists the seven major producers which in 1969 accounted for over 80 per cent of total crude steel production. In that year, Yawata and Fuji the two largest companies merged to form Nippon Steel, which in 1970 had a crude steel output greater than U.S. Steel Corp., thus becoming the world's largest producer. The major companies each produce a full range of steel products and qualities, including special steels. The smaller manufacturers concentrate upon light-rolled products (bars, rods, etc.) and special steels.

Japanese steel producers have not integrated mine ownership or distribution and metal-using operations into their activities. Of total industry shipments of finished steel products, 90 per cent are distributed by wholesalers (*ton'ya*). These organisation also undertake most of the marketing function for steelmakers, although this is gradually being absorbed by some of the larger producers.

The rapid growth and rationalisation of the industry in the post-war period has been achieved through a series of modernisation programmes, spanning the periods 1951–55, 1956–60 and 1960–65. In the first, the emphasis was placed upon the updating and expansion of existing plant and only one new plant was constructed, the Chiba Works of Kawasaki. Almost one-half of the total investments of the programme of $42 million were directed towards rolling operations which had been largely neglected before the war, and which were increasingly needed as the demand for flat-rolled products grew. Almost one-third of the capital requirements were provided in the form of loans through the help of the Government which also assisted the steel companies with tax concessions and other aid. Low interest loans from banks have also been important.

In the second and third plans, new plant construction became the prime objective, particularly with respect to the increase of iron and steel making capacity. Additional, in order to reduce the cost of imported materials (on which the Japanese industry is heavily dependent) to the lowest possible level, financial assistance was provided to other Asian countries for the development of new ore mines. Giant ore and coal carriers were constructed by consortia comprising the steel companies, the shipping industry and the Government, and long-term purchasing agreements were concluded. As the industry developed, dependence on Government finance decreased, and the proportion of investments from this source in the Second Programme fell to 11 per cent.[1]

The impact of the modernisation programmes has been substantial. Since the mid-1950s the average capacity of the larger firms has increased more than nine times, while that of plants has increased more than sixfold (Table 16). The effect on the distribution of capacity between firms and plants of particular sizes is shown in Table 32. By the late-1960s Japan had the highest concentration of steelmaking capacity in firms with capacities of 5 million tons or above of any of the countries of the enquiry. The US had a slightly higher concentration in plants in this size range, but as noted above, these are generally older facilities with smaller individual items of plant.

The expansion of the industry contributed to a rapid rise in labour productivity: crude steel output per man-hour increased $2\frac{1}{2}$ times between 1960 and 1967, faster than in any other country, offsetting the inflation of hourly earnings by a considerabl

1 Ibid., Table 23, p. 41.

Table 32 *Japan: Distribution of Crude Steelmaking Capacity by Size of Firm and Plant, mid-1950s and late-1960s*

Capacity Range (m. tons)	Firms		Plants	
	mid-1950s	late-1960s	mid-1950s	late-1960s
Below 0.5	28.2	3.0	46.2	5.2
0.5 – 0.9	14.4	2.9	32.7	4.6
1.0 – 1.9	36.3	1.6	–	11.6
2.0 – 4.9	21.1	7.2	21.1	43.4
5.0 and above	–	85.2	–	35.2
Total	100.0	100.0	100.0	100.0
Total capacity of estimates (m. tons)	12.3	70.6	12.3	70.6

Source: as for Table 18.

margin, and allowing unit labour costs to fall by a quarter (Table 15). High labour productivity has also been aided by close cooperation between management and the labour force.[1] Japanese companies offer workers employment for their lifetime and until recently employees have not been encouraged to move between companies. The security which this system provides has assisted the acceptance of new, more efficient, working systems by labour. It has the disadvantages that the labour force may not be effectively deployed and that labour costs tend to become a fixed charge to the company (apart from the large body of contractors' labour).

However, the industry is not without its problems, the most pressing being the lack of financial liquidity. In 1968 the long-term (bank) debt to equity ratio of the six largest steelmakers was 80:20 as compared with 43:57 for the member companies of the American Iron and Steel Institute,[2] This very high gearing contributes heavy interest charges which are insensitive to the level of output and this has been a prime cause of the importance which Japanese companies have placed upon maintaining capacity utilisation rates, with the attendant result of overproduction, causing erratic price and profit movements. (As noted, the influence of fixed costs is increased further by the system of labour recruitment).

In an attempt to stabilise domestic prices, in 1958 the Ministry of International Trade and Industry (MITI) sponsored the formation of the 'joint open sales system' (*Kokai Hanbai*). Under this, regular tripartite discussions take place between steel producers, distributors and MITI, as a result of which the steelmakers collectively determine their price structure, which covers 80 per cent of all ordinary steel products.[3] The Fair Trade Commission (FTC) has specially approved some of the aspects of this arrangement which restrict competition, and has simply ignored others. The price stabilisation programme has apparently not been as successful as those of other major steel producing countries.[4]

Ibid., pp. 133–5.

Ibid., Table 61, p. 127.

Ibid., pp. 103–4.

Ibid., p. 109.

Internationally, Japanese domestic prices became competitive during the 1960s, the prices for simple products reaching parity early in the decade, and those for more sophisticated products towards the end.[1] Published export prices on a free-on-board basis were generally below those of the USA and UK, but above those of the EEC during the 1960s,[2] and Kawahito, using a multiple regression analysis, found the delivered price differential to be the major determinant of the volume of Japanese steel imports into the US during the period 1959—68. Other contributing factors were the pressure of demand and the threat of labour troubles in the US.[3]

Until very recently, mergers have not been a feature of the Japanese industry. This is for two main reasons. During the initial period of post-war reconstruction, a system of antitrust regulation was established under American guidance which was, if anything, even more restrictive than its counter part in the US. it is administered by the Fair Trade Commission (F.T.C.).[4] Legislation and threats of intervention by the F.T.C. have discouraged mergers in many industries, including steel. A second factor has been the influence of the major banks. Each of the major steel producers secures most of its long-term loans from a particular bank. Thus Yawata, Fuji and Kobe are closely linked with the Industrial Bank of Japan, Nippon KKK with Fuji Bank, Kawasaki with Dai-ichi Bank, and Sumitomo is part of a financial holding by a bank of the same name.[5] The substantial and specialised bank involvement has been an impediment to merger and cooperation, since each bank is reluctant to re-linquish its controlling share of a major growth industry.

It is significant that the Yawata-Fuji merger in 1969 to create Nippon Steel involved two manufacturers with the same sponsoring bank. The amalgamation was approved by the F.T.C. only after lengthy discussion and consideration, but the growing surplus of capacity in the Japanese industry, together with increasingly harsh international competition and the rise of protectionist policies abroad un-doubtedly played a major role in obtaining Government approval.[6] The annual rate of growth of crude steel output slowed after the boom of 1967, and coupled with the development of increasingly larger steelworks (as the maximum output of BOS installations increased), this led to a fall in operating ratios. Two primary objects of the merger are to consolidate production on the largest and newest steelworks and to develop a strong, world-wide, sales network. Further cooperation between pro-ducers to plan and allocate investment is a strong possibility.

1   Ibid., p. 168.

2   Ibid., Table 56, p. 116.

3   Ibid., 149—183.

4   It is of course, no coincidence that a major agency of U.S. antitrust regulation has the same initials: The Federal Trade Commission.

5   "The Risen Sun", *The Economist,* supplement 3 June 1967.

6   *The Economist,* 28 June 1969, p. 78 and 1 November 1969, p. 75.

VII

The Evidence on Economies of Scale

In this section the sources and importance of economies of scale in the manufacture of steel are considered, first at the level of the individual works and then within entire companies. The final part considers the effect of inter-country variations in factor prices upon the extent of the economies of scale. The material collected and analysed is employed later in the enquiry.

An essential preliminary is a brief review of the general nature of economies of scale. Economies of scale are the reductions in average unit costs which may be associated with an increase in the scale of output of a good or service. Scale is a multi-dimensional notion, referring in the case of manufacturing activity not only to the rate of total output per period of time but also to such aspects as the total quantity of a particular good or goods produced (irrespective of time), the range of goods manufactured, the rate of output and the total production of each, the number of processes undertaken (i.e. the extent of vertical integration), and the number of separate establishments or plants operated.[1]

The economies of scale are achieved either through a reduction in the input of productive factors required to produce a unit of output, through a decrease in factor prices, or through a combination of both these effects, as scale is increased. Bain has termed the first of these responses *real* economies, and the second *pecuniary* economies.[2] Scale economies are derived from three main sources within economic activity: *technical, managerial and financial.* Mrs. Penrose has suggested that the first of the sources is associated principally, but not exclusively, with the scale of the individual plant, whereas the other two are associated chiefly with the firm.[3] In the present enquiry we are concerned primarily with technical economies of scale. Three principles, enunciated by Florence,[4] can be seen as giving rise to economies of scale. The first, the Principle of Bulk Transaction, refers to the tendency for certain elements in total costs to expand less than proportionately as the size of an operation is increased. The most usually quoted example of this is the relationship between the

---

1 The principal dimensions of scale in manufacturing activity are reviewed in A. Silberston, op. cit.,1972.

2 J.S. Bain, *Barriers to New Competition,* (Cambridge, Mass: Harvard University Press), 1956, p. 57.

3 E.T. Penrose, *The Theory of the Growth of the Firm,* (Oxford: Blackwell), 1959, p. 57.

4 P.S. Florence, *The Logic of British and American Industry,* (London: Routledge and Kegan Paul), revised edition, 1961, pp. 49–52.

capacity of a container — for example, a tank or a ship — and its cost of production. A given increase in the surface area of the container will increase its capacity more than proportionately, and production costs depend primarily upon surface area. The Principle of Massed (or Pooled) Reserves is derived from the statistical law of probability that the larger the number of values in a set, the smaller is their deviation likely to be around the mean, and relates to the reductions in the proportions of financial, inventory, equipment or labour reserves which may be possible as the scale of operation is increased. Finally, there is the Principle of Multiples, which states that there may be different optimal scales for different processes, and where these are integrated, the efficient scale of operation for the entire organisation will be determined by the lowest common multiple of the efficient scales of the various processes.

From the point of view of available literature relating to the sources and, particularly, to the extent of technical economies of scale, the steel industry is probably the best researched of all manufacturing activities. Listed chronologically, the most important investigations are those by Bain,[1] Stigler,[2] Weiss,[3] Pratten and Dean,[4] Shepherd,[5] Leckie and Morris,[6] and Pratten.[7] The first four enquiries have recently been summarised by Rowley.[8] In addition, some largely unsupported estimates of minimum output levels required for efficient operation are given in the Benson report.[9] In the following discussion, we consider the sources and extent of economies of scale in the three main processes in the industry (iron-making, steel-making, and rolling and finishing), and in entire plants. Finally we consider economies at the level of the firm. The analysis is based mainly upon the findings of the published enquiries, although we employ material we have obtained ourselves in the course of the present enquiry in order to supplement and clarify the results of other researchers, or to provide information in areas which have not previously been examined. We should perhaps make it clear that we have not felt it necessary as part of our present work to make a rigorous and thorough additional study of economies of scale.

1 J.S. Bain, op. cit., 1956.

2 G. Stigler, 'The Economies of Scale', *The Journal of Law and Economics*, October 1958, pp. 54–71.

3 L.R. Weiss, 'The Survival Technique and the Extent of Suboptimal Capacity', *Journal of Political Economy*, June 1964, pp. 246–261.

4 C. Pratten and R.M. Dean, op. cit., 1965.

5 W.G. Shepherd, 'What does the Survivor Technique show about Economies of Scale?', *Southern Economic Journal*, July 1967, pp. 113–122.

6 A.H. Leckie and A.J. Morris, 'Effect of Plant and Works Scale on Costs in the Iron and Steel Industry,' *Journal of the Iron and Steel Institute*, May 1968, pp. 442–52.

7 C.F. Pratten, op. cit., 1971, pp. 103–122.

8 C.K. Rowley, op. cit., 1971.

9 Development Co-ordinating Committee, op. cit., 1966.

(a) Iron Making

On the basis of data relating to 1962, Pratten and Dean[1] reported in 1965 that there were extensive economies of scale to be obtained in the production of pig iron in blast furnaces over an output range of from 0.1 to 1.0 million tons annually. The advantages came primarily from the opportunity to employ larger units of equipment as the scale of output was increased. The enquiry found no indications that the economies were necessarily extinguished at the upper end of the output range considered, although it was suggested that the expansion of the capacity of an individual blast furnace could not continue indefinitely, and the equipment would be duplicated at the highest annual output level of 1.0 million tons. The chief reason for this was claimed to be the unacceptable risk of disruption of the supply of hot metal for the subsequent steelmaking process which would be associated with a very large single furnace facility. Over the scale range considered, capital cost per ton of annual capacity for the largest installation considered (1.0 million tons annual capacity) was 46 per cent of that for the smallest (0.1 million tons). Unit operating costs exclusive of raw materials also fell with increases in scale, and for the largest facility were 75 per cent of the smallest. Similarly, unit labour costs, which are included in operating costs, formed 60 per cent of those of the smallest installation at the upper end of the capacity range. Pratten and Dean also quote data developed by the United Nations Economic Commission for Latin America (ECLA)[2] which showed (on the basis of factor prices in that area in the early 1960s), substantial economies of scale in pig iron production costs (net of materials) up to at least 1.5 million tons annually, although the rate of decline of unit costs reduced as scale was increased.

Reflecting technical opinion in the UK, the Benson Report[3] of 1966 emphasised the practical difficulties of pig iron production in a facility with less than two furnaces. The study suggested that, on the basis of best performances likely to be achieved in the mid-1970s a unit comprising two blast furnaces each with hearth diameters of 29 feet, would produce about 2.5 million tons of pig iron annually, and a unit with 31 feet diameter furnaces would produce about 2.8 million tons annually.

Pratten's most recent enquiry indicates that economies of scale in pig iron production run onto higher output levels.[4] On the basis of a detailed study by Leckie and Morris in 1968,[5] he reports that reductions in total unit costs (inclusive of materials) continue up to an annual output of 10 million tons. However, the rate of decrease is very slight in the range 5 to 10 million tons, and unit costs are elevated by only 4 per cent in a two-furnace facility to produce 2 million tons as compared with the largest plant. Subsequent developments have raised the minimum level of output necessary to avoid a severe cost penalty, since the maximum capacity of

1   C. Pratten and R.M. Dean, op. cit., 1965, pp. 65–7.

2   Economic Commission for Latin America, *Inter-regional Symposium on the Application of Modern Technical Practices on the Iron and Steel Industry in Developing Countries*, (New York: United Nations), 1964.

3   Development Co-ordinating Committee, op. cit., 1966.

4   C. Pratten, op. cit., 1971.

5   A.H. Leckie, and A.J. Morris, op. cit., 1968.

blast furnaces has been increased from 1 to at least 3 million tons, and recently a single-furnace unit has been installed in Japan with an annual capacity of 4.6 million tons.[1]

Given the present state of technology, it appears that an annual rate of pig iron production of about 3 million tons per furnace is necessary to achieve the bulk of the available economies of scale. Since installations require at least two furnaces to allow for re-lining, the necessary minimum output level for efficiency is about 6 million tons.

(b) Steelmaking

We indicated in Section III above that there are currently two feasible techniques for the production of crude steel in modern steelworks. The BOS appears able to produce common grades of crude steel at a low cost per ton of output, but requires a supply of hot metal (pig iron) and can take not more than one-third of its total charge in the form of cold scrap. The prohibitive cost of reheating cold pig for use in oxygen furnaces means that these facilities can only be operated in integrated plants which contain blast furnaces. The other available process is the electric arc furnace which can accept a metal charge composed entirely of cold scrap; thus it is employed in semi-integrated plants which lack iron-making facilities. The extent of the available economies of scale associated with these two techniques differs, and we consider them separately. The two other main techniques which are in use for crude steel production, the open hearth furnace and the basic bessemer (Thomas) converter, are both obsolete and are not considered further in this section. A review of the sources and extent of scale economies which are associated with them is given in Pratten and Dean.[2]

Considering the BOS, the Benson report indicated that, on the basis of an enquiry by a working party of the British Iron and Steel Federation, of the available versions, L-D facilities using low phosphorous iron ore would yield the lowest conversion and capital costs per ton of crude steel produced for plants with annual capacities of 1.5 million tons. Total annual costs in the other techniques ranged from 6.5 per cent above this for the L-D process using high phosphorous ore to 53.3 per cent above for the Kaldo process using high phosphorous ore. Total unit costs for the open hearth process were raised by between 38 and 51 per cent according to the particular variation of the technique considered.[3]

In their interim report Pratten and Dean indicated that substantial economies of scale were reflected in the decline in total unit costs (net of materials) as the annual capacity of L-D facilities was expanded. At an annual output of 1.0 million tons, total unit costs were 47 per cent of those at an annual output level of 0.1 million tons. The bulk of the savings came from capital economies, both through the expansion of individual vessel size, and through economies in construction and the provision of support facilities. Operating costs per unit of output also declined with increases in scale, although this tendency was not so marked as in the case of capital

1 Details of this installation were kindly provided by the Republic Steel Corporation.

2 C. Pratten and R.M. Dean, op. cit., 1965, **pp.** 68, 72.

3 Development Coordinating Committee, op. cit., 1966, pp. 38–9.

70

costs. The report also quotes the findings of an ECLA study which indicated the presence of scale economies at least to an annual output of 1.8 million tons.[1]

Since these enquiries, considerable technical improvements in the system have been achieved, and as a result scale economies may be expected to much higher levels than they indicated. The chief improvements have been an increase in individual vessel capacity, a reduction in scrap charging times, and an increase in blowing rates to allow the cycle time to be reduced to between 32 and 45 minutes.[2] On the basis of best-practice techniques in the mid-1960s, the Benson report suggested that the optimal capacity for individual L-D vessels was about 300 tons; for two-vessel works this indicated an annual output of about 3.5 million tons, and for a three-vessel works, about 6.8 million tons.[3] Since in any installation one converter is always out of operation for re-lining, the addition of a third converter allows annual output to be almost doubled.

More recently, the Commission of the European Communities has prepared estimates of the response of unit capital and operating costs to variations in the scale of two-and three-converter BOS facilities respectively. These are summarised in Table 33. Capital and operating costs are expressed relative to those for a three-converter installation to produce 7.7 million tons annually. The table shows that unit costs fall as the capacities of the individual converters are increased and that this tendency is most marked when two-converter facilities are considered. Above an annual output of about 2.6 million tons, unit costs are lowest in the three-converter facility; below this it seems likely that the two-converter unit will be preferable, because of the small individual converter capacity which would be necessary in a three-vessel installation.

Pratten[4] has up-dated Leckie and Morris's results to indicate the extent of economies of scale in integrated plants producing steel by the BOS route, and his results are summarised in Table 34. The irregular output levels which are considered occur because of the conversion from standard to metric tons. For each component of total costs, economies of scale continue up to an annual output level of about 10 million tons, although when total average costs are considered, the economies have mostly run out by 5 million tons. The reduction in the costs of materials as scale is increased results from the possibility that large tidewater plants can accept ore shipment in large bulk carriers. Additional data which he presents indicate more marked economies above an output of 5 million tons annually, as a result of further technological developments. These suggest scale-related cost savings for plants operated to Japanese levels of performance up to outputs of nearly 9 million tons annually. However, by UK and US present standards the main benefits are achieved at an output level of 6 million tons annually.[5]

1   C. Pratten and R.M. Dean, op. cit., 1966, pp. 72–3.

2   Development Coordinating Committee, op. cit., 1966, p. 40.

3   Ibid., pp. 40–41.

4   C.F. Pratten, op. cit., Table 12.2 p. 105.

5   Ibid. p. 107.

Table 33 *Indices of Unit Capital and Operating Costs in Two- and Three-Converter BOS at Various Annual Output Rates*

Converter Capacity (tons/heat)	Annual Output ('000 tons)	Indices of Unit Costs (3 × 300t converters = 100)	
		Capital	Operating
2-converter system			
100	1,280	208	127
200	2,560	158	112
300	3,840	134	106
3-converter system			
100	2,568	149	114
200	5,120	113	104
300	7,680	100	100

Source: Commission des Communautés Européennes, *Project de Memorandum sur les Objectif Généraux de la Sidérurgie de la Communauté pour les années 1975–80,* mimeo., 1971. Data are summarised from a study commissioned from Professor T. Schenck.

Table 34 *Indices of Average Annual Total Production Cost and its Components at Various Levels of Steel Output, Integrated Steelworks*

Annual Steel Output (million tons)	Indices of Unit Costs			
	Materials	Operating	Capital	Total
0.25	100	100	100	100
1.02	84	67	68	80
2.03	81	61	52	75
5.08	80	60	41	73
10.16	79	60	40	72

Source: C.F. Pratten, op. cit., 1971.

The extent of economies of scale is much less when steel is produced from scrap in electric furnaces. Pratten and Dean[1] indicated that the chief economies came from capital and operating savings associated with the size of individual furnaces and which continued at least to a standing capacity of 100 tons. Assuming that the furnace is tapped 40 times each week during 48 weeks in the year this suggests an annual output of 196, 000 tons. They also report, however, that the ECLA study found continuing economies for steel-melting shops employing a number of electric furnaces up to at least an annual output of 1.5 million tons.[2]

The Benson Report refers to a maximum furnace size of 152 tons and suggests an optimum output of 356,000 tons.[3] However, the maximum furnace size considered by Pratten in his most recent study is only 112 tons.[4] This indicates a minimum optimal annual output of about 214,000 tons, or 60 per cent of that indicated

1   C.F. Pratten and R.M. Dean, op. cit., 1965, pp. 70–1.

2   Ibid.

3   Development Coordinating Committee, op. cit., 1966, p. 40.

4   C.F. Pratten, op. cit., 1971, p. 117.

72

by the Benson Report, although Pratten's data indicate that the available economies have not completely run out at this scale of output.

The evidence on economies of scale associated with the BOS indicates that technical developments in recent years have contributed to a substantial (perhaps ten-fold) increase in the maximum annual output obtainable from complete (three-furnace) installations. Pratten's most recent estimates suggest that the economies for fully integrated plants run on at least to an output of 10 million tons annually;[1] however average total unit costs are up by only one per cent at one-half of this output rate. If we take as our indicator of minimum efficient scale (m.e.s.) the minimum annual output rate at which average costs fall by 5 per cent or less when scale is doubled, then the minimum output required appears to be about 2.0 million tons annually.

In the case of electric furnace production, undue emphasis has been placed in the literature on individual furnace size in indicating the extent of economies of scale. Economies are also to be expected in the construction of melting shops, the installation of equipment and the provision of services. Assuming a fairly narrow, standardised output of steel types and qualities, the economies may be expected to continue at least to the extent indicated by the ECLA enquiry[2] of 1.5 million tons annually, and recent technological developments may carry them beyond this, perhaps to 2.0 million tons annually.[3]

(c) Rolling and Finishing

The number and types of processes which follow the steel-making stage depend upon the required form of the final product. In each of the countries of our enquiry the vast majority of total output by weight (in most cases about 95 per cent) is of hot rolled products, some of which are subjected to further cold rolling and other finishing processes. In this section we consider only these classes of goods. In general the evidence we have reviewed indicates that, for most of the rolling and finishing processes, recent technological developments have brought about substantial increases in the minimum efficient scales of operation, and that the available economies of scale are closely connected with the capacity of individual items of equipment (rolling mills, etc.). In examining progressively larger integrated hot and cold strip mills, Pratten and Dean[4] found reductions in capital charges, labour input, and heat consumption per unit of finished product as scale increased.

Rolled products fall into two broad categories: flat-rolled, which includes sheet, strip and plate; and other rolled, which embraces bars, rods, heavy and light sections and so on. For these processes, the crude steel from the melting shops must be in the form of oblongs of particular dimensions, known as billets and slabs.[5] Until recently,

---

1   Ibid., Table 12.2 p. 105.

2   Economic Commission for Latin America, op. cit., 1964.

3   This probably applies also to special steel production where the range of products is not very large and where fairly long production runs can be obtained. Pratten (op. cit. 1971, p. 118) makes the same point, but does not provide any quantitative evidence.

4   C. Pratten and R.M. Dean, op. cit., 1965, p. 75.

5   An indication of the usual dimensions of these is given in Appendix 1.

all crude steel was tapped from the melting furnace or converter and cast into ingot moulds. When solid, the ingots were re-heated and passed through a primary mill to be reduced to billets, or slabs. This process still accounts for 98 per cent annually of all rolled products in the UK, and the proportions for the other countries are similar. Pratten's data suggest that the optimum size for a primary mill is large relative to most other subsequent rolling operations. He reports that the largest actual or contemplated facilities in the world are of the order of 4.6 million tons for a slabbing mill, and 4.1 million tons for a blooming mill.[1] However, some increase in the technical maximum has apparently occurred since these data were collected; the Commission of the European Communities[2] reports a maximum annual capacity for a slabbing mill of 6 million tons. Leckie and Morris indicate that on the basis of prices ruling in the mid-1960s, a 45-inch universal slabbing mill with an annual capacity of about 3.5 million tons would cost $32.88 million, or $9.36 per ton of installed capacity.[3]

Since the early 1960s, much research in most steel industries has centred upon the development of a commercial system of continuous casting to by-pass the ingot and primary rolling stages. In this process, molten steel is passed into a vertical tube, solidifies, and is withdrawn from the other end and cut into the required lengths. Pratten and Dean,[4] in considering early forms of continuous casting machinery, note that the technique has the advantages that impurities are reduced, wastage rates are very low, and considerably below those incurred with traditional primary rolling; the primary rolling stage is by-passed, and capital equipment expenses are relatively low. They suggest that most of the available economies of scale are achieved at an annual output of around 120,000 tons. A year after their study, the Benson Report[5] was suggesting that systems yielding 500,000 tons annually were commercially viable, and that future expansion was highly likely. Pratten's latest enquiries[6] show that the largest systems contemplated or installed have annual capacities of one million tons. Despite its apparent advantages, the introduction of the continuous casting technique has generally been slow in most of the steel industries we have considered. The chief reasons for this appear to be the difficulty of integrating the technique which requires a continuous *flow* of molten metal, with the BOS system which produces large *batches* of metal, and the generally low quality of steel cast. However, according to one of our respondents in Belgium, these problems have been largely overcome by the McLouth Steel Corp. of the US, and a widespread expansion of the use of the process is likely in the near future.

Turning to flat-rolled products, the most substantial increase in maximum technical capacity appears to have occurred in the production of wide strip and sheet.

1   C.F. Pratten, op. cit., 1971, p. 109.

2   Commission des Communautés Européennes, op. cit., 1971, p. 153.

3   A.H. Leckie and A.J. Morris, op. cit., 1968, Table III, p. 450.

4   C. Pratten and R.M. Dean, op. cit., 1965, p. 74.

5   Development Coordinating Committee, op. cit., 1966, pp. 42–3.

6   C.F. Pratten, op. cit., 1971, p. 109.

Pratten and Dean[1] report data relating to the late 1950s which indicate a maximum annual output of 1.3 to 2.5 million tons for a continuous facility producing hot-rolled strip, but in the later report Pratten indicates an output of 6 million tons.[2] The maximum for narrow and medium strip has remained constant at around 0.5 million tons.[3,4] Cold rolling mills, for subsequent processing of strip and sheet, have current technical maximum annual capacities of about 2.0 million tons.[5] For the production of plate (other than that rolled in strip mills), the Benson Report[6] indicated an annual output of between 0.75 and 1.0 million tons according to type, but Pratten[7] increases this to 2.4 million tons. In most cases, therefore, the minimum efficient scale for the production of a narrow range of the main types of flat-rolled products is large, both absolutely and, more importantly, relatively to the total outputs of many of the steel-producing countries. However, the full benefits of the large items of equipment can only be fully achieved when they are fully loaded, and when the range of products to be manufactured is not extensive. Countries (or firms) with extensive demand fluctuations may find it better to duplicate smaller items of equipment, and vary the number in operation. Similarly, roll changes to produce products of different dimensions are costly both of time and labour, and mill duplication may again be a solution. Against this, however, technical improvements are enabling large rolling mills to become more flexible. A new strip mill installed by the Republic Steel Corporation at its Cleveland, Ohio, works has 82-inch rolls, but can roll all widths down to 14 inches.

The required annual outputs for the efficient rolling of light-rolled products are considerably below the levels indicated so far. According to a respondent in the U.S. industry this is chiefly because scale-sensitive costs (capital and labour) form a lower proportion of total costs in bar, rod and section rolling than in flat rolling, mainly as a result of fewer, and simpler, stages in the process. The Benson report[8] indicated required annual outputs ranging from 0.30 million tons for a light section and bar mill, to 0.65 million tons for a four-stand wire rod mill. Pratten[9] suggests a range of between 0.6 and 1.0 million tons, and this is confirmed by the findings of the Commission of the European Communities.[10] Leckie and Morris's investigation[11] indicated that the capital cost per ton of annual capacity for secondary

1   C. Pratten and R.M. Dean, op. cit., 1965, p. 75.

2   C.F. Pratten, op. cit., 1971, p. 109.

3   Development Coordinating Committee, op. cit., 1966, p. 42.

4   C.F. Pratten, op. cit., 1971, p. 109.

5   Ibid.

6   Development Coordinating Committee, op. cit., 1966, p. 42.

7   C.F. Pratten, op. cit., 1971.

8   Development Coordinating Committee, op. cit., 1966.

9   C.F. Pratten, op. cit., 1971.

10 Commission des Communautés Européennes, op. cit., 1971, p. 153.

11 A.H. Leckie and A.J. Morris, op. cit., 1968, Table III, p. 450.

rolling mills ranged from $28.0 for a 80-inch hot rolling mill, producing 3.3 million tons annually to $67.20 for either a 12 ft. tandem plate mill producing 1.0 million tons, or a bar mill producing 0.25 million tons.

With the exception of tube and pipe manufacture, subsequent finishing processes have fairly low minimum efficient scales. Tinplate production consists of a series of successive processes in which steel coil is prepared and electrolytically tinned. On the basis of the state of present knowledge, respondents in the UK suggested to us that an annual output of about 60,000 tons would secure most of the available economies of scale. Each stage in the process contributes a relatively small proportion to total costs, and hence the scope for scale economies is limited.[1] Similar results are to be expected for galvanising.

The scale of output required for efficient tube production depends very much upon the technique of production employed. In continuous welding, the tube is formed from a hot metal strip and the weld is made longitudinally by rolling one opposing edge over the other. The technique is used mainly for the production of general purpose tubes with diameters not exceeding six inches. An annual output of about 0.5 million tons must be attained, and long runs of tubes of a given diameter are essential. Electric resistance welding has been used until recently for the production of high precision tubes, but is now being extended into the manufacture of cheaper qualities. The tube is formed longitudinally from cold metal, and the opposing edges of the metal are fused by the passing of an electric current. In UK installations, tube is delivered at the rate of 200 feet per minute, a rate much slower than that for the continuous weld process, but a very large diameter tube is rolled, which is then stretched to reduce it to the required diameter and thickness of wall. The final rate at which the tube is delivered approaches 1000 feet per minute, and an annual output of around one million tons is probably necessary for the efficient production of general purpose tubes. Tubes with diameters of six inches or above are produced in the UK by spiralling strip (although continuous weld techniques are occasionally employed in the US). An annual output of 0.5 million tons seems likely to collect most of the economies.

The preceding discussion indicates that, generally, the minimum efficient scale of rolling operation is set by the very large capacity of the primary mill. With the exception of sheet and wide strip production, integrated steel works require to duplicate their secondary rolling mills; the large scale of the operation relative to the

1   A breakdown of the costs of a ton of tinplate produced in a U.K. works in 1970 is as follows:

	£	%
Cost of coil from steel works	49.50	76.4
Cost of tinplate manufacture:		
Pickling	1.75	2.7
Straightening	2.60	4.0
Cleaning	1.35	2.1
Annealing	3.40	5.3
Tempering	1.75	2.7
Coil preparation	1.75	2.7
Tinning	2.65	4.1
Total	64.75	100.0

size of the market in most countries means that plants which do not produce strip and/or sheet are invariably multi-product units.[1] For strip and sheet production, the capacity of the best-practice secondary, hot-rolling, mill is currently greater than that of the primary mill, but this need not raise the necessary scale of primary rolling because sufficient billets can be purchased to make up any short-fall.

It is possible for small-scale steel-melters and rollers to overcome some of the problems which the large annual capacity of the rolling operation implies. The "mini-mills" which have developed to the greatest extent in the US generally employ continuous casting units and concentrate upon the production of reinforcing and merchant bars in which the maintenance of a consistent quality is not important. Another way is to sub-contract primary rolling to a larger producer, and then provide the subsequent hot rolling and finishing processes. During our US fieldwork we visited a stainless steel company in which this arrangement was apparently working well, but other respondents told us that it was not a typical feature of the industry. A third way is to use second-hand equipment.

It is important to note that our conclusions on economies of scale in rolling and finishing apply at least as forcefully to special as to common steel production. In fact the available economies may be more extensive because capital and labour costs are usually proportionately more important.[2] In most countries, small-scale special steel producers survive because the market to which they cater is also small and they are required to produce a range of products. In the US Allegheny-Ludlum, a special steel manufacturer, has expanded to produce over 2 million tons in 1970, yielding *a priori* evidence of substantial scale economies.

(d) Entire Plants

In addition to the economies of scale reviewed so far, there are further benefits which relate both to the overall output of plants and to their degree of integration. Pratten and Dean[3] note that the cost of handling raw materials is an important component of total costs, and that fairly substantial reductions in unit costs are to be expected as scale is increased, the precise magnitude of the savings depending on the method of transport employed. They also indicate economies as integrated plants are expanded through increases in the sizes of coking facilities and oxygen equipment, through the opportunities for more efficient co-ordination by management, and through reductions in transport and re-heating expenses.[4]

This is not to suggest, however, that non-integrated plants are *necessarily* at a severe disadvantage. Pratten[5] points out that in certain cases, reheating expenses may be offset by an improvement in quality and a reduction in rejection rates which are made possible through the opportunity to inspect the semi-finished metal in a cold state. Also small steel-melting and rolling works which are entirely scrap-based

1 cf. Development Co-ordinating Committee, op. cit., 1966, p. 42.

2 cf. C.F. Pratten, op. cit., 1971, p. 117.

3 C. Pratten and R.M. Dean, op. cit., 1965, pp. 77–8.

4 Ibid., pp. 78–9.

5 C. Pratten, op. cit., 1971, p. 116.

can be located close to the source of their raw material, which is usually also the primary market for their finished products. In this way unit transport costs, both of raw materials and of the finished products, can be substantially reduced as compared with an integrated tide-water facility using imported ore and supplying a dispersed market.

It will be clear from the discussion so far that the minimum efficient scale of plant for the manufacture of steel products depends both upon the process by which the crude steel is produced and upon the product mix of the final total output. Hence we may expect several output scales to be optimal according to the technical and market factors assumed. Until recently it was generally assumed that for flat-rolled products the large minimum annual capacity of the rolling facilities effectively determined the overall scale of plants, but Pratten's recent evidence suggests that on-going economies in the BOS may carry the required scale for an integrated plant beyond this.[1]

In Table 35 we have collected recent estimates of minimum efficient plant size. They are grouped according to the degree of integration and the product-mix assumed, and within each group the results are arranged chronologically. The estimates have been made using either the *cost-engineering* technique or the *survivorship* method. In the first, estimates of the response of the components of total production costs to variations in the scale of hypothetical new facilities are obtained from industry respondents with relevant knowledge and experience. There are a number of methods by which minimum efficient scale can be identified from the results. One way is to take that scale of output at which all the economies are achieve However, frequently average unit costs appear to continue falling with increases in scale, although at a reducing rate, almost indefinitely, and m.e.s. may then be taken as the minimum scale at which unit costs fall by a set percentage or less when scale is further doubled.[2] Another approach is to take the scale of the current best-practice plant.[3] Because Leckie and Morris assumed the product-mix of their plants to alter with scale, it was not realistic to take a minimum or near-minimum average unit cost point as an indicator and they used the first major return-on-investment peak instead.[4] The effect of this is to provide a lower m.e.s. than would obtain through an examination of the cost data alone. In the second method, census and other data are examined to discover which size-classes of plants (measured usually by employment) are tending to maintain or increase their total outputs, either absolutely or relative to their industries as a whole, through time. The smallest plant scale which is found to be holding its absolute or relative output is then taken as the m.e.s. The advantages and disadvantages of these approaches have been

1   Ibid., p. 105.

2   This technique is used by C.F. Pratten, op. cit., 1971 and by the present author, *Economies of Scale in the Brewing Industry*, unpublished dissertation for the degree of M. Phil. of Leeds University, 1971, Chapter I.

3   See F.M. Scherer, op. cit., 1971.

4   A.H. Leckie and A.J. Morris, op. cit., 1968, p. 443.

considered by Pratten and Dean[1] and, more recently, by Rowley;[2] Shepherd[3] has provided a brilliant critique of the survivorship test.

As might be expected, the table shows that m.e.s. is generally found to be higher in integrated as compared with semi-integrated plants. In the case of integrated plants producing flat-rolled goods, the m.e.s. has apparently increased sharply through time, and this is, of course, wholly reconcilable with what we know about recent changes in steel-melting and rolling technology. The range of values for integrated plants producing other rolled products appears to occur chiefly because of the rather different method of identifying the m.e.s. employed by Leckie and Morris (see above) as compared with those of the other investigators. For semi-integrated plants producing other rolled products, Pratten's recent low estimate, which is almost equal to that of Bain 15 years earlier, indicates the sensitivity of costs to the location of the plant relative both to the market for the final product and to the availability of scrap.

With the exception of the estimate by the Commission of the European Communities, it seems that on the basis of the evidence available so far the present minimum efficient scale for the production of both flat and other rolled products in fully integrated plants is in the region of 4.0 million tons annually. For other rolled products manufactured in integrated plants without blast-furnaces and using electric arc furnaces the m.e.s. appears to lie between 0.1 and 1.0 million tons according to market and technical conditions.

While the evidence available from published and other sources gives some impression of the minimum efficient scales of operation for the production of particular combinations of products under certain technical and commercial conditions, it does not give any indication of the *slope* of the scale curve at outputs below m.e.s. For our subsequent analysis of the extent to which the available scale economies are in practice achieved in the countries of our enquiry, it is essential to obtain some impression of the general rate of change of average unit costs as plant scale is varied, and we attempt this in the following paragraphs.

There are currently two "best-practice" techniques available — the BOS and the Electric Arc. To simplify the analysis we consider the first in the context of an integrated plant making hot-rolled sheet only, and the second in connection with a semi-integrated plant making bars only. Table 36 shows estimates of the components of total production costs at selected output scales for integrated plants. The source and methods of calculation of the data are given in the footnotes. It should be noted that the use of a constant scale coefficient (of 0.56) for the calculation of unit operating costs in rolling most probably overestimates the importance of the economies of scale in that section. This is because the coefficient was calculated using cost data spanning an output range of from 0.7 to 3.0 million tons annually, whereas the maximum scale considered in the table is 5.0 million tons, and it is likely that the coefficient would have a higher value as outputs of this order are approached (i.e. scale economies would be reduced). Against this effect, however,

1 C. Pratten and R.M. Dean, op. cit., 1965, pp. 21–4.

2 C.K. Rowley, op. cit., 1971, pp. 50–1.

3 W.G. Shepherd, op. cit., 1967.

Table 35 *Estimates of Minimum Efficient Scale of Steelworks in terms of Annual Crude Steel Production*

Production Route and Product-Mix	Minimum Efficient Scale (million tons of crude steel per annum)	Source and Date of Estimate	Basis of Estimate
Blast and Steel Furnaces/Flat and Other Rolled	4.0 and above	Pratten, 1971 (UK)	Engineering estimates
Blast and Steel Furnaces/Flat Rolled	1.0 − 2.5	Bain, 1956 (US)	Engineering estimates
	3.0 and above	Pratten and Dean, 1965 (UK)	Engineering estimates
	4.2	Benson, 1966 (UK)	Engineering estimates
	4.0	Leckie & Morris, 1968 (UK)	Engineering estimates
	8.0	Commission des Communautés Européennes, 1971 (E.E.C.)	Engineering estimates
Blast and Steel Furnaces/Other Rolled	3.0	Benson, 1966 (UK)	Engineering estimates
	1.5	Leckie and Morris, 1968 (UK)	Engineering estimates
	4.0	Commission des Communautés Européennes, 1971 (E.E.C.)	Engineering estimates
Steel Furnaces/Flat Rolled	0.5 − 1.0	Bain, 1956 (US)	Engineering estimates
Steel Furnaces/Other Rolled	0.1 − 0.5	Bain, 1956 (US)	Engineering estimates (applies also to special steel)
	1.0 − 1.5	Benson, 1966 (UK)	Engineering estimates (light rolled products)
	1.25	Leckie and Morris, 1968 (UK)	Engineering estimates (billet and medium-section mills)
	about 0.15	Pratten, 1971 (Germany, F.R.)	Engineering estimates
Unspecified	0.76	Stigler, 1958 (US 19 -51)	Survivor technique; converted from percentage share of total industry capacity.[a]
	0.8	Saving, 1961; Weiss, 1964 (US, 1947−54 census data)	Survivor technique; converted from employment data[b]
	2.25	Weiss, 1964 (US 1948−60)	Survivor technique; capacity data.

80

Notes:

(a) The estimates indicate that minimum efficient plant size was 0.75 per cent of total industry ingot capacity in 1951. The conversion is based on a total industry ingot capacity in 1950 of 90.2 tons (see Committee on Finance, US Senate, op. cit, 1967, Table A-18, p. 269).

(b) The enquiries gauge minimum efficient scale in terms of employment and suggest a plant size of 500 persons. This represents 0.1 per cent of the labour force classified to the census industry group in 1954. Using employment as a proxy for output, this indicates an annual plant output of 800,000 tons (total industry output was 80 million tons).

Sources:

J.S. Bain, op. cit., 1956, p. 236.

G. Stigler, op. cit., 1958, p. 50.

T. Saving, 'Estimation of Optimum Size of Plant by the Survivor Technique', *Quarterly Journal of Economics*, Vol. LXXV, No. 4, Nov. 1961, pp. 569–607.

L.R. Weiss, op. cit., 1964, pp. 249 and 258.

C. Pratten and R.M. Dean, op. cit., 1965, pp. 80–1.

Development Co-ordinating Committee, op. cit., 1966, pp. 43–5.

A.H. Leckie and A.J. Morris, op. cit., 1968, p. 445.

C. Pratten, op. cit., 1971, pp. 112, 122.

Commission des Communautés Européennes, op. cit., 1971, p. 155.

Table 36 *Effect of Scale of Crude Steel Output upon Unit Costs, by process and type of cost, fully integrated plants, producing hot-rolled strip UK.*

Process and Items of Cost	Annual Output of Crude Steel (million tons)			
	0.1	0.5	1.0	5.0
	Cost per ton ($)			
Steelmaking				
capital[a]	7.06	4.39	3.62	2.38
index	297	185	153	100
operating[b]	20.40	9.36	7.94	7.15
index	285	131	111	100
total	27.46	13.75	11.56	9.53
index	288	144	121	100
Rolling				
capital[c]	222.41	44.50	22.25	4.82
index	4610	922	461	100
operating[d]	142.20	30.79	22.68	11.16
index	1274	276	203	100
total	364.61	75.29	44.93	15.98
index	2281	471	281	100
Total				
capital	229.47	48. 89	25.87	7.20
index	3187	679	359	100
operating	162.60	40.15	30.62	18.31
index	888	219	167	100
raw materials[e]	61.94	61.94	61.94	61.94
index	100	100	100	100
total	454.01	150.98	118.43	87.45
index	519	173	135	100

Sources and Notes: The data in this table are derived principally from A.H. Leckie and A.J. Morris, op. cit., 1968, pp. 442–52. Dr. Leckie has kindly provided additional information allowing steelmaking costs to be estimated for the particular scales considered in the table, and to allow for inflation since the original calculations were prepared. Annual capital charges are taken as 15 per cent of the original total investment, and represent depreciation at 5 per cent and interest at 10 per cent annually. The exchange rate is £ = \$2.40. In acknowledging Dr. Leckie's help I would emphasise that his assistance has been confined to the estimation of capital charges and those operating costs which are affected by scale. The detail of the table should be taken as indicating trends only and not the costs to be encountered in actual plants.
(a) Calculated using the formula $K = [n.135000M^{\frac{2}{3}} + 95Q + 2140Q^{\frac{2}{3}}] i$

where: K = total capital cost in £;
n = number of furnaces in installation;
M = vessel standing capacity in tons;
Q = weekly throughput of installation in tons;
and i = an inflation multiplier with a value of 1.16.
Values of parameters are:

Annual capacity (million tons)	Q	M	n
0.1	1942	9	2
0.5	9710	44	2
1.0	19420	87	2
5.0	97100	217	3

and assume 45 minutes tap to tap time, 51.5 working weeks per year.

(b) Calculated using the formula $R_q = \left[\dfrac{n(178000 + 2200M)}{Q} + 34 \right] i$

82

the assumption that unit raw material costs remain constant as scale alters serves to underestimate the available economies.[1] The calculations indicate that total unit production costs, inclusive of raw materials, rise very sharply as the scale of output falls below 1.0 million tons annually.

Since the data in the table indicate the magnitude of unit costs at only a few points in a very wide range of scales, they do not give any precise indication either of the m.e.s. or of the elevation of unit costs at particular fractions of m.e.s. The findings of Table 36 have been developed in an attempt to indicate the behaviour of total unit costs as plant scale is expanded from 0.1 to 10.0 million tons annually, and the results are given in Table 37. Using total costs at output scales of 1.0 and 5.0 million tons in Table 36 we have calculated a scale coefficient, using the method stated in footnote (d) to the table, and have employed this to estimate unit costs at the levels of output up to 10 million tons annually which are not given in Table 36. Table 37 indicates that, on the basis of our estimates, the available economies of scale have run out at an annual output of 10 million tons. The index for an output of 11 million tons is 99.7, and we may assume that for practical purposes, unit costs remain constant at output levels above 10 million tons.

As we have indicated above, one useful definition of m.e.s. is that output level at which unit costs first decrease by a specified percentage or less when scale is further doubled. A useful arbitrary indicator to take for this purpose is 5 per cent, and this suggests an m.e.s. of 8 million tons annually. This is exactly comparable with the results of the recent study by the European Communities Commission (Table 35), and is substantially higher than the other estimates considered in the table. Unit costs are shown to be elevated by 13 per cent at one-half m.e.s., somewhat above Pratten's estimate using a smaller m.e.s.[2] At one-quarter m.e.s., unit costs are up by 30 per cent.

where: R_q = operating cost per ton of product in shillings;
n = number of furnaces *operating* and is equal to $n - 1$ in (a) above;
and Q and i (= 1.25) have the same definitions as in (a) above.

(c) Equipment requirements are a 45 inch universal slabbing mill; slabbing furnaces; an 80 inch hot strip mill, and finishing facilities. Capital costs are obtained from A.H. Leckie and A.J. Morris, op. cit., Table II (Part II), p. 447 adjusted for subsequent inflation ($i = 1.16$).

(d) For these calculations, a "scale coefficient" (n) for operating costs in the production of hot-rolled strip was derived from A.H. Leckie and A.J. Morris, op. cit., Table II (Part II), p. 447. This shows that at the smallest weekly output level considered, 13,800 tons of ingot (Y_1), hot-rolled strip operating costs are £6.14 million annually (X_1). When the strip mill is fully developed at 77,500 tons of ingot weekly (Y_2) operating costs are £16.16 million annually (X_2). The scale coefficient is then calculated using the formula:

$$n = \log \frac{X_2}{X_1} \Bigg/ \log \frac{Y_2}{Y_1}$$

This has a value of 0.56 and can be used to indicate operating costs for any value of X. The cost data in the table are adjusted for inflation ($i = 1.25$).

(e) Obtained from Table 11. No allowance is made for any economies of scale in pig iron production which may be available.

1 See C.F. Pratten, op. cit., 1971, Table 12.2, p. 105.

2 An 8 per cent elevation with a m.e.s. of 4.0 million tons. See C.F. Pratten, op. cit., 1971, Table 12.4, p. 122.

Table 37 *Indices of Total Unit Production Costs (inclusive of raw materials) in integrated Plants of particular scales producing Hot-Rolled Strip*

Scale of Plant (million tons of crude steel annually)	Index of Total Unit Costs (10.0 million tons = 100)
0.1	593
0.5	197
1.0	155
2.0	136
3.0	126
4.0	119
5.0	114
6.0	110
7.0	107
8.0	105
9.0	102
10.0	100

Source and Notes:

Data are derived from Table 36. Indices for scales not shown in that table are estimated, using a scale coefficient of 0.81, derived from data for output scales of 1.0 and 5.0 million tons. The method of calculation for the scale coefficient is given in note (d) to Table 36.

A further refinement of the notion of minimum efficient scale is to consider that output level at which unit costs are elevated by a specified percentage above those at m.e.s. itself. This output level can usefully be termed "reasonably efficient scale" (r.e.s.) and recognises that plants and firms can survive at scales somewhat less than those at which unit costs are minimised because, for example, the ability to survive in the market is not affected by small percentage variations in costs, and because the disadvantages of small scale can to some extent be offset by improvements in the level of managerial or X-efficiency. If r.e.s. is defined as that scale of output at which unit costs are 5 per cent above those at m.e.s., the table shows it to have a value of 6 million tons, an output which is much more easily reconcilable with the other estimates reviewed in Table 35.

There is some reason to suppose that the results of Table 37 tend to over-state both the extent and the importance of economies of scale, and if this is in fact the case, our conclusions about m.e.s., r.e.s., and the degree to which average unit costs are elevated at output levels below m.e.s. will also be over-estimated. The scale economies may be shown in the table to continue to too high a level because of the use of a scale coefficient which obtains between annual outputs of from 1.0 to 5.0 million tons to estimate costs at output levels in excess of 5.0 million tons. It is probable that the appropriate coefficient for these scales is significantly above 0.81, which is the value employed, particularly since section (c) above has indicated that hot-strip rolling mills have a maximum annual capacity of about 5.0 million tons. As total plant output increases above this, it will be necessary to duplicate the rolling facilities, causing unit rolling costs to rise initially and then to decline as scale is raised to the point at which the additional equipment is fully utilised. The effect of this in checking the rate of decrease of total unit costs as scale is increased appears to be fairly important, since Table 36 shows that at an annual output of 5.0 million tons, rolling costs form 18 per cent of the total. Hence the scale at which the economies of scale in plants producing hot-rolled strip are absolutely extinguished is probably below the level indicated in Table 37, and this is almost certainly true when the production of other-rolled products (bars, rods, etc.) is considered, where the maximum capacities of mills are below that for hot-rolled strip. However, the indication of the table may be more accurate when the joint production of flat- and other-rolled products is considered.

The scale coefficient employed may also exaggerate the slope of the scale curve as indicated by Table 37; on the other hand, our calculations do not incorporate the effects of any economies of scale in pig iron production which are available for integrated plants.

Bearing these qualifications in mind, the estimates of m.e.s., r.e.s., and the slope of the scale curve developed above for integrated plants producing hot-rolled strip may be accepted as being tolerably accurate, and we employ them in our comparative analysis of the efficiency of the structure of the steel industry in VIII below.

Turning to scrap-based, semi-integrated plants using electric arc technology and producing bars, the estimated responses of total unit cost and its components to scale variations are shown in Table 38. Again, the methods employed in the preparation of the estimates are detailed in the footnotes to the table. As compared with the integrated plants considered in Table 36, the economies of scale are both less marked and less extensive. For steel-making, the available economies continue to an output of 2.5 million tons annually, but are mostly achieved at an annual output of 1.0 million tons. For rolling all the economies are achieved as soon as a single mill of 250,000 tons annual capacity is fully utilised, and unit costs remain constant as scale is expanded above this output level. Total unit cost, inclusive of scrap costs, continue to decline to an annual output of 2.5 million tons, but are up by only two per cent at an output of one-fifth this level (0.5 million tons). There is little reason to suppose that the scale economies continue beyond the upper output limit considered in the table.

It is clear from the total unit cost index in Table 38 that the m.e.s. and the r.e.s. for semi-integrated plants will be somewhere between annual outputs of 0.1 and 0.5 million tons. The scale coefficient between these two points, estimated by the method described in the appropriate footnote to Table 36, has a value of 0.94; this suggests that if total unit costs at an output of 2.5 million tons are 100, costs at 0.2, 0.3 and 0.4 million tons will be 108, 106 and 104 respectively.

(e) Company-Level Economies

In this section we consider the factors which may cause the minimum efficient scale for a steel-making company to exceed that for an individual plant. One such factor is the possibility that there may be advantages for companies associated with the operation of more than one plant. We have commented in the previous section that for integrated plants producing hot-rolled sheet, total unit costs cease to decline with further increases in scale at an annual ingot output of about 10 million tons, but that there is no reason to suppose that diseconomies of scale operate (causing unit costs to rise) over a wide range of outputs above this level, given the absence of management difficulties. Hence in theory a firm could expand its output above this

Table 38 *Estimates of Unit Costs at Particular Outputs of Crude Steel, by Process and Type of Cost, Semi-integrated plants producing bars only U.K.*

Process and Class of Cost	Annual Crude Steel Output (million tons)			
	0.1	0.5	1.0	2.5
	Unit Costs ($)			
Steel Making				
Capital[a]	5.62	4.10	3.74	3.43
– index	163.6	119.6	109.1	100.0
Operating[b]	22.18	17.52	16.73	16.58
– index	133.7	105.6	100.9	100.0
Total	27.80	21.62	20.47	20.01
Rolling				
Capital[c]	25.06	10.03	10.03	10.03
– index	250	100	100	100
Operating[d]	18.00	18.00	18.00	18.00
– index	100	100	100	100
Total	43.06	28.03	28.03	28.03
– index	154	100	100	100
Total				
Capital	30.68	14.13	13.77	13.46
– index	228	105	102	100
Operating	40.18	35.52	34.73	34.58
– index	116	103	100	100
Raw materials[e]	36.82	36.82	36.82	36.82
– index	100	100	100	100
Total	107.68	86.47	85.32	84.86
– index	127	102	101	100

Source: as for Table 36.

Notes: (a) Calculated using the formula $K = [n. 49400 \, M^{\frac{2}{3}} + 108Q + 2640 \, Q^{\frac{2}{3}}] \, i$ where the terms have the same definitions (and i has the same value) as in footnote (a) to Table 36.

Values of parameters are:

Annual Capacity (million gross tons)	Q	M	n
0.1	2083	52	1
0.5	10415	130	2
1.0	20830	180	3
2.5	52075	186	7

and assume approximately 40 taps a week, 48 working weeks a year. Annual depreciation and interest are calculated at 15 per cent of the original investment.

(b) Calculated using the formula $R_Q = \left[\dfrac{n. \, 108000}{Q} + 96 \right] i$

where R_Q = operating cost per ton of product in shillings; n and Q have the same values as above, and $i = 1.25$. Depreciation and interest are calculated as above.

(c) Assumes combinations of bar mills with individual capacities of 0.25 million tons annually and with capital costs of £6 million each.

(d) Operating costs for a bar mill of 0.25 million tons annual capacity.

(e) Obtained from Table 11.

level, and widen its product range, in a single plant without suffering any unit production cost increases.

Taking a wider view than this restricted consideration of the production cost-scale connection, and relating the argument more specifically to conditions in the real world, it is likely that there probably are some further advantages for companies associated with multi-plant operation. In the first place, rising transport costs per unit of output are likely to set an upper limit to plant size. For oxygen and electric arc technology plants alike, unit out-shipment costs seem likely to rise beyond some output scale as the market area supplied is widened and the areal density of consumers decreases, causing a reduction in the volume of shipments per mile. When added vertically to the unit production cost curve, which we suggest is characteristically L-shaped, the rising unit transport cost curve will cause the total unit cost curve also to begin to rise *at some scale*. The point at which this occurs will depend upon individual circumstances, and will vary from plant to plant. Specifically it will be influenced by the relative importance in total costs of production and transport expenses, the scale of output at which unit transport costs begin to rise, and the slope of the production cost curve over its descending portion.[1] To obtain a valid indication of the check which out-shipment costs exercise upon maximum plant scales detailed research is required, for which time in the present programme has not been available, but on the basis of our international interviews with respondents we are sure that the scale at which unit production-plus-distribution costs are minimised is not below plant m.e.s. when production costs alone are considered. At what scale *above* m.e.s. the point lies we have no idea, but it seems likely that it will vary from country to country, and in geographically extensive nations like the U.S. and Canada, between regions, according to the characteristics of the market. In these conditions, multi-plant operation can enable companies to increase their scale of output without incurring the penalty of increasing total unit costs through rising unit transport expenses. For scrap-based electric arc plants, rising unit transport costs of scrap obtained from the region surrounding the plant may exercise a similar check on the maximum feasible scale of output. This effect is probably less important for oxygen plants because bulk shipments of iron ore can be achieved.

A second factor is that operating several plants may enable companies to adjust more easily to the cyclical variations in production which we have seen to be characteristic of most, if not all, the countries of the enquiry. Where facilities vary both in size and in vintage, producers will be able to operate their newest and largest plants at a fairly constant rate near full capacity, accommodating demand fluctuations largely through varying the output from their smaller and older plants.

Thirdly, the disruptive effects of strikes or breakdowns may be proportionately greater in a single-plant company than in a multi-plant organisation at the same scale of output, and this may introduce a preference in favour of the latter. Fourthly, the existence of two best-practice technologies, each with its particular and different m.e.s., and with different locational requirements, is likely to lead large companies towards multi-plant operation. Fifthly, where incremental increases in productive capacity are both large and expensive, multi-plant operation, coupled with trans-

---

1 A more detailed, though sadly data-starved, consideration of this problem is provided in my *Economies of Scale in the Brewing Industry,* op. cit., 1971, Chapter 5.

shipment of final products between regional markets may enable more rational planning of investment and the elimination of surplus capacity.

A final point is that when companies expand through merger, the increase in the number of plants controlled improves the flexibility of production scheduling, allowing a greater concentration of the manufacture of particular classes of goods upon specific plants, thus providing the advantages of longer production runs, and enabling surplus capacity in sub-optimal plants to be eradicated more quickly. These are potentially large advantages for the British Steel Corporation,[1] and similar advantages have been achieved by producers in several of the other countries of our enquiry. For example, the merger of Cockerill-Ougrée with Providence in Belgium in 1966 has enabled the production of particular classes and sizes of flat-rolled products to be allocated more efficiently between the rolling mills.

These factors suggest that, other considerations apart, advantages from multi-plant operation are likely to carry the minimum efficient scale of companies beyond that for individual plants. We have no estimates of the impact of these advantages upon total costs (and given the complex nature of the problem, it would be difficult to obtain such information), but the implication is that unit costs at company level continue to fall up to a scale equal to perhaps twice the plant m.e.s. for integrated works producing hot-rolled strip (i.e. of the order of 16 million tons annually). However, the rate of decline of unit costs is probably slight: Bain's interview data indicate that a firm of m.e.s. could operate between 1 and 8 plants of efficient scale, and that unit costs would be between 2 and 5 per cent lower than in a single plant of m.e.s.[2]

In addition to these economies, Pratten suggests that there are further benefits accruing to large companies from at least three further sources.[3] Forward vertical integration can ease the market penetration problem, and, by yielding realistic forecasts of demand, can reduce cyclical production fluctuations.[4] Research and development expenditure can be spread over a larger output. The marketing effort can be better organised and coordinated both at home and in international markets.

The difficulties in estimating the m.e.s. for companies and the slope of the scale curve at outputs below this level is reflected in the paucity of information in published and other studies as compared with that for plants. Using the survivorship test, Stigler estimated that in the US in 1950, lowest unit costs companies had annual capacities of between 2.5 and 25 million tons.[5] More recently, Rowley infers constant returns to scale for companies with capacities of from 6 to 30 million tons.[6] The Commission of the European Communities suggests that for efficiency a fully-integrated company in the EEC needs an annual capacity of about

1 cf. C.F. Pratten, op. cit., 1971, p. 119.

2 J.S. Bain, op. cit., 1956, Table IX, p. 86.

3 C.F. Pratten, op. cit., pp. 119–20.

4 These fluctuations, arising from over-ordering and cancellations by customers, can be severe, at least in the U.K. See Christopher Blake, op. cit., 1965, pp. 62–80.

5 G Stigler, op. cit., 1958, p. 57.

6 C.K. Rowley, op. cit., 1971, p. 56.

12 million tons for the production of flat-rolled products (plate and sheet).[1] Again, this last estimate compares favourably with our own indications based on the benefits forthcoming from multi-plant operation and we employ it in Part VIII. The m.e.s. for a semi-integrated company manufacturing rods and bars seems likely to be identical with that for the single plant (between 0.3 and 0.4 million tons annually).

(f) International Variations in Minimum Efficient Scale

Minimum efficient scale has been defined above as the smallest level of output which, when doubled, results in a fall in average unit costs of 5 per cent or less. The analysis so far has indicated that the m.e.s. is sensitive to the assumptions made about the technical conditions of manufacture and the product-mix. Our estimates have been prepared in terms of the prevailing factor costs in the UK, and this raises the question of whether variations between countries in factor prices will significantly influence the m.e.s.

Two effects are possible. The first will occur if the proportion of total costs formed by each main component varies between the countries. Since economies of scale result almost entirely from savings in unit capital and operating expenses, the smaller is the share of each in total costs, the slower will be the rate of decline of total unit costs as scale is increased. In other words, the *slope* of the scale curve will be affected, and thus the m.e.s. (as defined) will differ from country to country. The second effect relates to the *position* of the scale curve. The lower are the costs of the factors of production, the lower will be the location of the scale curve, and if factor prices differ between countries, the scale at which average unit costs are elevated five per cent above m.e.s. in the lowest-cost country will vary between them. This implies that, in terms of international competitive ability, industries in low-cost countries seem likely to be able to tolerate a greater proportion of relatively small-scale plants or firms than their higher cost competitors.

To indicate the effect of inter-country cost differences on the slope of the scale curve we have weighted appropriately the components of the total cost index given in Table 36. In the absence of any contrary evidence, we have assumed that capital and raw material costs are identical between the various countries, and are as shown in the table, but we have endeavoured to indicate inter-country differences in operating costs. To do this we have taken the UK operating costs for the plant of 1.0 million tons capacity (= $30.62) from Table 36 and assumed that the unit operating costs at the same scale of output in the other countries stand in the same relation to this figure as do their unit labour costs to the UK figure in Table 14. This assumption appears to be a valid one because labour expenses are typically a major component of total operating costs in the steel industry. For example, Table 13 shows that in the UK wages and salaries are 86 per cent of operating costs, where these are defined as net output less depreciation and net trading profit before tax.

On the bases of these estimates, sets of weights for each country are obtained as shown in Table 39. It is clear that the greatest difference in the slope of the scale curve will occur in the case of Italy where the weights diverge the most from those for the UK. In Table 40 the weighted index of total unit costs for Italy is compared

---

[1] Commission des Communautés Européennes, op. cit., 1971, p. 160.

Table 39 *Derivation of Weights for Components of Total Unit Costs for Integrated Plants with Annual Crude Steel Capacities of 1.0 million tons producing hot-rolled strip, by Country*

Country		Unit Cost Component			
		Capital	Operating	Materials	Total
Belgium-Luxembourg	– unit cost ($)	25.87	11.94	61.94	99.75
	– weights	26	12	62	100
France	– unit cost ($)	25.87	9.49	61.94	97.30
	– weights	27	10	64	100
Germany, F.R.	– unit cost ($)	25.87	10.72	61.94	98.53
	– weights	26	11	63	100
Italy	– unit cost ($)	25.87	6.43	61.94	94.24
	– weights	27	7	66	100
Netherlands	– unit costs ($)	25.87	7.66	61.94	95.47
	– weights	27	8	65	100
UK	– unit costs ($)	25.87	30.62	61.94	118.43
	– weights	22	26	52	100
US	– unit cost ($)	25.87	30.62	61.94	118.43
	– weights	22	26	52	100
Canada	– unit cost ($)	25.87	26.64	61.94	114.45
	– weights	23	23	54	100
Japan	– unit cost ($)	25.87	10.72	61.94	98.53
	– weights	26	11	63	100

Sources: Tables 14 and 38

Table 40 *Estimated Weighted Indices of Average Total Unit Costs at Selected Output Scales, Plants producing Hot-rolled Strip. Italy and UK*

Output scale (million tons)	Average Unit Cost Index (5 million tons = 100)	
	Italy	*UK*
0.1	446	519
0.5	163	173
1.0	129	135
5.0	100	100

Sources: Tables 36 and 39.

with the index for the UK. It is apparent that the differences in the importance of the factor prices causes total unit costs in Italy to rise more slowly, but except at the level of the smallest plant, the divergence is not great. The indication is that at scales in excess of 5 million tons annually, and in which range m.e.s. lies, the difference in the slopes of the scale curves for each country caused by factor price variations is not significant and in any case is almost certainly not greater than the errors in the estimates. This conclusion also appears to hold in the cases of integrated plants producing a range of rolled products, semi-integrated plants rolling bars and rods, and entire companies.

Table 39 shows that at 1 million tons annual capacity there are marked differences in total unit costs between the countries. If the cost index developed in Table 37 is applied to these figures, the total unit costs at each output scale between 1 and 10 million tons in each country can be estimated. The results are displayed in Table 41. The estimates indicate only the differences between the countries in the

Table 41 *Estimated Total Unit Production Costs for Integrated Plants producing Hot-rolled Strip by Annual Capacity and Country*

	Annual Capacity (million tons)									
	1.0	2.0	3.0	4.0	5.0	6.0	7.0	8.0	9.0	10.0
	Unit Costs ($)									
Belgium-Luxembourg	99.75	87.78	80.80	76.80	73.81	70.82	68.83	67.83	65.83	64.84
index	156	137	126	120	115	111	107	(106)	103	101
France	97.31	85.63	78.82	74.93	72.00	69.09	67.15	66.17	64.22	63.25
index	152	134	123	117	112	108	(105)	103	100	99
Germany, F.R.	98.53	86.70	79.81	75.87	72.91	69.96	67.99	67.00	65.03	64.04
index	154	136	125	118	114	109	106	(105)	101	100
Italy	94.24	82.93	76.33	72.56	69.73	66.91	65.03	64.09	62.20	61.26
index	147	130	119	113	109	104	101	100	97	96
Netherlands	95.46	84.00	77.33	73.50	70.64	67.78	65.87	64.92	63.01	62.05
index	149	131	121	115	110	(106)	103	101	98	97
UK	118.43	104.22	95.94	91.20	87.64	84.09	81.72	80.53	78.17	76.98
index	185	163	150	142	137	131	128	126	122	120
US	118.43	104.22	95.94	91.20	87.64	84.09	81.72	80.53	78.17	76.98
index	185	163	150	142	137	131	128	126	122	120
Canada	114.46	100.73	92.71	88.14	84.70	81.26	78.97	77.83	75.54	74.40
index	179	157	145	138	132	127	123	121	118	116
Japan	98.53	86.70	79.81	75.87	72.91	69.96	67.99	67.00	65.03	64.04
index	154	135	125	118	114	109	106	(105)	101	100

Source: Tables 37 and 39.

position of the scale curve, and ignore differences in the slope of the curve. In Italy (the lowest-cost nation) m.e.s. is seen to be an annual capacity of 8 million tons; if the costs at this scale are taken as equal to 100, and all other costs are related to them, it is a simple matter to identify from the indices the output scales in the other countries at which unit costs are about 5 per cent higher. In the table the indices which indicate that unit costs are elevated by about the appropriate amount are ringed. Where the five per cent elevation point lies between two outputs, we have ringed the higher value in cases where the appropriate point is mid-way between the outputs, and have ringed the closest value in other instances.

It is immediately apparent that with the exception of the UK, the US and Canada the appropriate indices correspond to capacities which are very close to 8 million tons. In other words, for these countries differences between them in factor prices do not affect their respective competitive abilities, given that all capacity is in plants of minimum efficient scale. But for the UK, the USA and Canada, if it is assumed that constant returns to scale obtain at outputs above 10 million tons, unit costs are *always* substantially more than five per cent above those at m.e.s. in Italy.

This analysis suggests that for the nations of the sample cross-country differences in operating costs do not influence substantially either the slope or the position of the scale curve over most ranges of output. However, differences in capital costs have been ignored. Burn showed that for chemical process plants capital costs per unit of capacity in Japan could be upto 25 per cent less than those for comparable facilities in the US.[1] If this maximum difference is assumed to hold for the steel industry, the data of Tables 39 and 41 can be reworked to determine the sensitivity of the results to variations in capital costs. The influence on the contribution of capital to total costs is very slight, but the effect on the absolute level of total costs, and thus upon the position of the scale curve, is more marked. A 25 per cent reduction in capital costs in Japan would reduce total costs to 75 per cent of those in the US, a fall of almost ten percentage points as compared with the outcome of Table 41.

Thus differences in capital costs are likely to affect the international competitiveness of nations, but in general factor cost variations do not influence the minimum efficient scale of output. It will therefore be convenient to disregard the effect of international cost variations in the subsequent analysis.

1 D. Burn, op. cit., 1971.

VIII

Economies of Scale and International Structural Variations

In this section, we endeavour to indicate the extent to which the available economies of scale are in fact realised in the steel industries of the several countries of the enquiry, and also the effect on this degree of attainment of changes in minimum efficient scale and in the structure of the industry since the end of the 1950s. We consider first the main production processes, then integrated plants, and finally entire companies.

(a) Processes

Under this head we include pig iron production in blast-furnaces, crude steel production and hot rolling. For pig iron production, Table 6 provided partial data showing the average sizes of blast furnaces in 1960 and 1968. Pratten and Dean's results suggest scale economies at least to 1.0 million tons capacity for a facility with two furnaces of 0.5 million tons each, with total unit costs up an estimated 32 per cent in a single furnace facility with a capacity of 0.1 million tons.[1] On this basis, Table 6 suggests that in 1968 iron production in the US and Canada, where average furnace capacity was 0.5 million tons, was very efficient provided (as is fairly likely) most furnaces were used in tandem. The efficiency level was slightly lower in Belgium-Luxembourg followed by the UK and France. If the estimate of the degree of elevation of unit costs at sub-optimal scales is correct, France with an average furnace output of only 0.2 million tons, must pay a fairly high penalty. In each of the countries, average furnace size rose between 1960 and 1968; as technological developments probably also raised minimum efficient scale during that period, it seems likely that each industry at least maintained its relative efficiency.

For common grades of steel the oxygen system is the most efficient technique currently available. However, Tables 7 and 8 showed that in 1968 this process accounted for more than one-half total output in only the Netherlands and Japan. The principal reasons which limit the speed with which the technique can be introduced include the amount by which total industry output increases each year (if this is small in relation to the m.e.s. for the technique, new facilities will be built only occasionally); the existence of equipment which although obsolete has not yet reached the end of its useful life, and the presence of certain market or regional characteristics which favour another technique. This last reason operates where the electric arc process is appropriate because of the importance of special steel or the plentiful supply of scrap, or, as in France, where the presence of high-phosphorus

1   C. Pratten and R.M. Dean, op. cit., 1965, pp. 65–7.

ores maintains the Thomas process. Bearing these qualifications in mind, Tables 7 and 8 provide a very crude impression of the relative efficiencies of the industries on the basis of the extent to which they incorporate "best-practice" technology. Japan ranks first, with the Netherlands second, followed by Belgium-Luxembourg, Germany F.R. and the U.S.A. (equal third); Italy, the UK and France. The available data are not sufficiently detailed to permit Canada to be ranked.

A further comparison of relative efficiencies can be made by considering the proportion of total oxygen steel-making capacity in each country contained in facilities of m.e.s. or above. Pratten's findings reviewed in VII(b) above indicated that the economies of scale for oxygen systems have almost run out at a capacity of 5 million tons, and that m.e.s. (using a 5 per cent indicator) was 2 million tons. Data prepared by Kaiser Engineers show that only Japan and Germany, F.R. possessed BOS facilities with capacities of 5 million tons or above in 1971: Japan had four such installations, of which the Fukuyama No. 2 shop of Nippon K.K. with an annual capacity of almost 7 million tons was the largest, while there were two installations in Germany, F.R., both operated by Thyssen, the annual capacity of the largest of which was 6 million tons. However, if we take a benchmark of 2 million tons capacity as a minimum criterion for efficiency, there are qualifying installations in each country, and the relative efficiencies are as shown in Table 42. According to this, the highest degree of efficiency is in the Netherlands, where all oxygen capacity is in installations with capacities of 2 million tons or more, and the lowest degree is in Belgium-Luxembourg, where optimally-sized units contribute 37 per cent of total oxygen capacity.

Table 42 *Percentage of Total Oxygen Steel-Making Capacity in Units of Efficient Scale by Country, 1971*

Country	BOS Capacity (million tons)		
	Total Installed	Total in Units with capacities of 2.0 m. tons or above	Percentage in efficient units $\frac{\text{Col. 3}}{\text{Col. 2}} \times 100$
Belgium-Luxembourg	11.4	4.0	36.8
France	6.6	3.8	57.9
Germany, F.R.	35.2	29.9	84.8
Italy	10.7	8.5	79.7
Netherlands	4.8	4.8	100.0
U.K.	13.9	5.3	38.5
U.S.	71.0	50.4	71.0
Canada	4.0	2.5	63.3
Japan	96.1	80.7	83.9

Source: Kaiser Engineers, *L-D Process Newsletter,* (Chicago), October 1971.

With respect to electric arc technology, data on average furnace capacities have been obtained only for the UK. In 1968 of 192 furnaces only 34 (18 per cent) had heat capacities of 30 tons or more, suggesting annual capacities of 58,000 tons and above, while 81 (42 per cent) had heat capacities of less than 5 tons, suggesting annual capacities of under 10,000 tons.[1] In his recent study, Pratten shows economie

1 B.S.C., *Annual Statistics, 1968,* (London), 1969. Estimates of annual capacity assume 40 taps a week during a 48-week year.

94

of scale continuing at least up to a furnace heat capacity of 110 tons,[1] and thus even allowing for the importance of special steels in the UK, and the variety of qualities and types within that category, furnace capacity is clearly very small.

The vast majority of capacity for hot rolling in each country is contained in plants with steel-making facilities, and since rolling-mill capacities (especially for primary rolling) frequently determine the m.e.s. for entire plants, the plant size-distribution findings considered in (b) below provide a rough guide to the overall efficiency of rolling in each industry, and we do not anticipate them here. However, in addition to the variations between the nations in the importance of plants capable of supporting efficient rolling facilities, there are also differences in product-mix, and the length of production runs. The minimum annual output to allow the efficient production of light and heavy rolled products is less than that for flat-rolled products; hence all else equal, countries in which the former are relatively important components of total output should be able to tolerate smaller units. From Table 2 we might expect this effect to operate chiefly in Belgium-Luxembourg, France, Germany, F.R., the Netherlands and Italy. As to production runs, our impression from our discussions is that the North American countries and Japan are able to roll greater volumes of given product classes than the other nations. This results both from their larger average plant sizes and from their efforts at rationalisation to reduce the range of types and sizes of product produced.

We are not able to comment on inter-country differences in the efficiency of cold rolling and finishing processes, since these are diverse and have differing, though generally small minimum efficient scales.

(b) Plants

A major problem in endeavouring to indicate and compare for each country the proportion of total steel-making capacity contained in efficient plants is that while the generally prevalent m.e.s. for integrated works may be fairly easily specified, plants of a much smaller scale may operate efficiently because of the existence of particular technical, demand, or locational characteristics. These have been considered above, and include the use of scrap in electric furnaces, the requirements for special steels, and the presence of raw materials of a quality suited to a technique which is not appropriate elsewhere. To overcome this difficulty we have subtracted from total capacity the amount contained in small-scale plants in each country, and expressed that in plants of efficient scale as a proportion of the remainder; in the following we refer to this recomputed measure as *reckonable capacity*.[2]

For the measurement of recent efficiency levels (i.e. for the late-1960s) we have calculated reckonable capacity by deleting capacity in plants of less than 1 million tons; this appears justifiable on the grounds that in VII (d) we found the available economies of scale in modern semi-integrated plants to have virtually run out at this level, and the m.e.s. to lie between 0.3 and 0.4 million tons.

A further problem arises at this stage in connection with the minimum scale of

1   C.F. Pratten, op. cit., 1971, p. 117.

2   I am grateful to Professor F.M. Scherer for the initial idea which prompted this line of approach.

output to be selected at or above which plants are taken as efficient. In VII (d) we suggested that on the basis of engineering cost estimates, the m.e.s. for an integrated steelworks producing hot-rolled sheet was of the order of 8 million tons. According to this, of the countries of the enquiry only the US has any plants of efficient scale, with the five qualifying works contributing 23 per cent of adjusted capacity. Such an efficiency criterion gives no indication of the relative efficiency (or inefficiency) of the remaining countries. If the boundary is reduced to 6 million tons (which we found to be the r.e.s. at which total costs were raised 5 per cent above their level at m.e.s.), efficiency ratings can be computed for three countries: the US has 34 per cent of adjusted capacity in efficient plants, with Japan having 22 per cent and Germany, F.R. 18 per cent. In order to obtain a rating (other than zero) for all nine countries, the minimum boundary must be reduced to 2.5 million tons, or one-third of the m.e.s. Table 37 indicates that at this scale unit costs in BOS plants are elevated by about 25 per cent above those at m.e.s. and our classification includes plants using open-hearth and other obsolescent techniques, whose unit costs will be elevated even more; thus our analysis includes as efficient, plants which are high-cost by an standard.

The results using this criterion are shown in column 3 of Table 43. Four of the nine countries (the Netherlands, Canada, the US and Japan) obtain ratios of above 60 per cent, and can be rated as *highly efficient.* Germany, F.R. and Italy can be rated as *moderately efficient,* with ratios of between 40 and 60 per cent, while the remainder (UK, France and Belgium-Luxembourg must be graded as *inefficient.* This grading is qualified slightly by two factors. The first is the higher degree of product specialisation at plant level in the continental European nations as compared with the UK (although not, apparently, in comparison with the US, Japan and Canada). This factor (which depends *inter alia* on managerial choice) serves to increase the gauged efficiency of Germany, F.R., Italy, France and Belgium-Luxembourg. The second factor is the cyclical variations in output which might require some countries to maintain obsolescent small-scale plants in operation to cater to the peaks in demand. Appendix 2 shows in fact that the cyclical fluctuations are most marked for those nations which have the lowest proportions of total capacity in reasonably efficient plants, and this may modify slightly their adverse ratings.

Employing a similar approach, comparative ratios for the mid-1950s are given in column 2 of the table. Here the minimum efficiency boundary has been taken as 1 million tons, or one-half of the estimated m.e.s. for integrated plants which prevailed at that time. This boundary thus stands in roughly the same relation to the prevailing m.e.s. as does the boundary for the late-1960s enquiry, and, assuming the scale curve rises fairly sharply below the m.e.s., enables us to maintain the classification of some fairly high-cost plants as efficient. The m.e.s. of 2 million tons is the scale suggested to us by industry respondents at which most of the available economies would be attained in modern open-hearth steel-making units; this technique accounted for the majority of steel output in all the countries of the enquiry save France and Belgium-Luxembourg in the mid-1950s, as Tables 7 and 8 show. For the two exceptions, the Basic Bessemer (Thomas) process was dominant, but there is no reason to suppose that the m.e.s. for that technique is substantially different from that for the open-hearth process. The Economic Commission for Europe found in their 1962 report that total unit costs (inclusive of capital) for the Thomas process fell as scale was raised to 1.5 million tons, but at that level most of the available economies had been achieved.[1] Additional support of our choice of m.e.s. is provided by Burn's indication that towards the end of the 1950s a continuous hot-strip mill would produce about 2 million tons.[2]

Table 43 *Estimated Efficiency Ratios for Integrated Steelworks, mid-1950s and late-1960s, by Country*

| Country | Estimated Efficiency Ratios | | Efficiency Change Index |
	mid-1950s[a]	late-1960s[b]	(col. 3/col. 2)
Belgium-Luxembourg	38.77	27.17	70
France	65.26	27.44	42
Germany, F.R.	n.a.	52.67	n.a.
Italy	37.53	42.67	114
Netherlands	98.80	100.00	101
U.K.	81.50	32.71	40
U.S.A.	89.17	81.52	91
Canada	81.06	90.31	111
Japan	39.22	76.33	195

Notes:
    (a) Capacity in plants of 1.0 million tons and above as percentage of that in plants of 0.5 million tons and above.
    (b) Capacity in plants of 2.5 million tons and above as percentage of that in plants of 1.0 million tons and above.
Source: Section VI.

Reckonable capacity for the mid-1950s analysis has been calculated by excluding capacity in plants below 0.5 million tons in size. A lower cut-off point than in the late-1960s analysis is necessary both because of the lower minimum efficiency boundary, and because the efficient operation of semi-integrated plants in the scale range from 0.5 to 1.0 million tons was probably inhibited in the early post-war period by the high cost of electricity, a relative shortage of scrap, and the state of technical knowledge. With the exception of Canada a higher proportion of capacity is excluded in the mid-1950s analysis than in that for the late-1960s, but the ratio of the cut-off point to the minimum efficiency boundary is approximately the same in both enquiries.

Column 2 of Table 43 presents the results of the mid-1950s analysis for eight of the countries. Using the same broad classification as above, the Netherlands, the US, the UK, Canada and France are rated as *highly efficient,* with the remainder receiving *inefficient* gradings. The main interest of this outcome lies, of course, in the comparison with the late-1960s analysis. Column 4 of the table relates the later ratios to the earlier ones and shows clearly that in the decade and a half of the enquiry, in one-half the cases for which complete data are available, it has not been possible for the industries to maintain their proportions of reckonable capacity in efficient plants as m.e.s. has risen. The most marked reductions in rated efficiency have occurred in the UK, and in France. In the remaining cases, the proportion of reckonable capacity in efficient plants has increased, and this improvement has been

  Economic Commission for Europe, op. cit., 1962, Table 28, p. 69.

  D. Burn, op. cit., 1961, p. 648.

substantial in Japan. We consider the implications of this in X below.

(c) Companies

We adopt the same approach as in the previous sub-section for the assessment of the relative efficiencies of the steel industries in terms of company size. The total reckonable capacities for the dates of the two analyses are unchanged inspite of the fact that generally a smaller proportion of *total* (unadjusted) capacity is contained in small units (below 0.5 and below 1.0 million tons for the mid-1950s and the late-1960s respectively) when firms are considered in place of plants. The capacity in small *firms* must be excluded on the premise that they may be efficient through catering to localised markets, but on the same basis so must the capacity in small *plants* which are owned by larger companies. Hence for the two analyses we exclude in effect all capacity in small plants.

This points the way to a further problem. In preparing our efficiency ratios we need to select a boundary to indicate the minimum capacity at which firms can be regarded as efficient. But firms may satisfy this overall scale criterion by operating one or more plants with individual capacities lying below the boundary. We do not attempt to correct for this inconsistency in the ensuing analysis, and it should be borne in mind that as a result our company-level efficiency ratings for each date are likely to be over-estimates.

For the company analysis we have taken the same minimum efficiency boundaries as in the previous sub-section (1.0 and 2.5 million tons respectively for the mid-1950s and the late-1960s). Our reasoning for this is as follows. We suggested in VII (e) above that the current m.e.s. for an integrated company producing a wide range of rolled products including sheet steel was of the order of 12 million tons. On this basis only the US and Japan have companies which qualify as efficient, contributing 61 and 53 per cent respectively of reckonable capacity, and the boundary has to be reduced to 3 million tons to collect positive ratings for each country. Since this is only slightly above the boundary for the plant analysis, it is tempting to adopt the latter; the ratings then suggest not only the relative efficiency differences between the countries at company level, but also the *potential* efficiency rating which could be obtained if the firms classified as efficient had all their capacity in plants of m.e.s. or above. The ratings can then be linked to the results of the plant efficiency analysis to indicate the role of multi-plant operation in reducing the efficiency levels of the industries below the possible maximum. In the case of the mid-1950s analysis, we have no reliable evidence of the prevailing firm m.e.s., and we can avoid overstating this by using that for individual plants; if we follow the plant analysis and select a minimum boundary equal to one-half m.e.s. we allow the inclusion of most companies other than those which on the basis of scale must be very high-cost, and as with the analysis for the later date we can provide an indication of the efficiency potential of the company structure.

Table 44 shows the company efficiency ratios for the two dates, and indicates the degree of change which has taken place between them. The striking feature is that in every country in the late-1960s the proportion of total reckonable capacity in fairly large companies was very high indeed — the lowest rating (for Italy) is 72 per cent. The curious rating for France of over 100 per cent arises because through the operation of small plants, the capacity contained in firms of sufficient scale to be rated as efficient exceeds the total adjusted capacity. With the exception of Italy, the high efficiency levels were also present in the mid-1950s. In contrast with the plant analysis of Table 43, the general tendency in the period between the two analyses has been for the efficiency levels to rise — the sole exception is the US. It is clear from the earlier discussion that for the European countries this increase has been due in large part to mergers.

Table 44 *Estimated Efficiency Ratios for Integrated Steel Companies, mid-1950s and late-1960s by Country*

Country	Estimated Efficiency Ratios		Efficiency Change Index
	mid-1950s[(a)]	late-1960s[(b)]	(Col. 3/col. 2)
Belgium-Luxembourg	80.3	85.5	106
France	88.1	108.6	123
Germany, F.R.	n.a.	73.0	n.a.
Italy	48.7	72.2	148
Netherlands	n.a.	100.0	n.a.
U.K.	89.8	99.1	110
U.S.	94.2	89.3	95
Canada	81.1	90.3	111
Japan	79.9	99.1	124

Notes:
(a) Capacity in companies of 1.0 million tons and above as percentage of that in companies of 0.5 million tons and above.
(b) Capacity in companies of 2.5 million tons and above as percentage of that in companies of 1.0 million tons and above.
Source: Section VI.

Table 45 *Ratio of Assessed to Potential Efficiency for Steel Plants, mid-1950s and late-1960s, by Country*

Country	Assessed/Potential Efficiency Ratios		Percentage Points Change, mid-1950s–
	mid-1950s	late-1960s	late-1960s
Belgium-Luxembourg	48.2	31.8	−16.4
France	74.1	25.3	−48.8
Germany, F.R.	n.a.	72.2	n.a.
Italy	77.1	59.1	−18.0
Netherlands	n.a.	100.0	n.a.
U.K.	90.8	33.0	−57.8
U.S.	n.a.	91.3	n.a.
Canada	100.0	100.0	0
Japan	49.1	77.0	+27.9

Source: Tables 43 and 44.

The role of multi-plant operation in reducing the economies of scale available to large firms is indicated sharply in Table 45. Here for each country on each date the plant-level ratios of Table 43 are shown as percentages of the corresponding company-level ratios of Table 44. For the late-1960s, the shortfall between the proportion of total adjusted capacity contained in companies capable of supporting at least a single plant of 2.5 million tons and the proportion of total capacity actually contained in such plants is in some cases dramatic — France, Belgium-Luxembourg and the UK realise no more than one-third of their potential efficiency. The final column of the table shows for those countries for which the data are available the change in the degree to which the potential plant-level economies were in practice realised between the two dates. In four of the five cases, the ratio of assessed to potential efficiency has declined through the period. For Belgium-Luxembourg and France, it is again noticeable that this reduction has occurred during a period in which extensive mergers have taken place, indicating that considerable plant-level rationalisation is necessary before the full benefits can be achieved. The data for the UK refer to the pre-nationalisation period, and thus yield no such implications.

These comments refer to the overall scale of steelmaking in firms. Differences between the countries in the degree of vertical integration are not great and do not appear to affect the efficiency ratings very much. Backward integration into ore winning and processing confers very little advantage, and may indeed sometimes be a positive disadvantage, as for some of the European manufacturers, when the world price of ore falls below that at which their own captive mines can produce it. With the exception of the UK (and possibly also of Japan), the various industries are responsible for the greater part of the stockholding and distribution of their products to customers. As we have noted, this apparently improves the communication between purchaser and manufactures and alleviates the amplification of the demand cycle at the production stage. There is clearly room for improvement in this respect in the UK.

IX

International Differences in Structure and Performance

(a) Scope and Method

The final part of the analysis considers the role of structural differences between the industries in influencing their performances. The performance of an industry is a multi-dimensional concept which it is impossible to gauge adequately in terms of a single indicator. The available measures generally fall into two main groups, financial and physical. The first group includes costs, prices and profit rates. Cost data are not generally directly available. Efforts have been made to use prices as a proxy for costs[1] but the main draw-backs for a small-scale study such as ours are the difficulties of obtaining sufficient data to allow a product-weighted industry average to be prepared; of deciding whether to employ domestic market or export prices (in the steel industry the latter are usually substantially lower than the former); of allowing for freight and tariff charges, and of discovering the extent to which actual prices (net of discounts, rebates, etc.) differ from the list prices. The main problem in the use of profit rates is that they are generally available only for the quoted public companies in each country; they are not directly comparable because of inter-firm and inter-industry variations in activities and accounting practices, and they are seriously affected by a multitude of other factors, of which, in the steel industry, the existence of protected home markets and Government price regulation can be very important.

The physical indicator group takes in productivity levels, output growth rates and trade performance. Crude measures of labour productivity do not reflect differences between plants, firms and industries in the ranges of products manufactured and activities undertaken. Overall productivity indicators, which include the efficiency of capital are difficult, if not impossible, to develop. Output growth is substantially influenced by conditions in the domestic market, where specific tariff protection and the overall rate of economic expansion may be important.

Trade performance, however, is an attractive indicator. The notion of a connection between industrial efficiency and trade performance has its roots in the theory of relative advantage. It may be expected that, all else equal, nations with higher efficiency levels in a given industry, relative to industry in general, would register higher export sales for that industry than their relatively less efficient competitors. Several factors will operate to distort this tendency, of which the most important are tariffs, freight charges, the degree of price discrimination between home and export markets, and the prevailing rates of currency exchange, which may not be

Cf. J. Singer, op. cit., 1969, especially pp. 30–2.

in equilibrium. For our analysis we have related, first, the measured efficiency levels of the steel industries in the late-1960s to their subsequent export performance and, secondly, the rates of change of the efficiency levels between the mid-1950s and the late-1960s to the corresponding rates of change of export performance.[1]

We define export performance as the share of each country in the total exports of all the countries in the sample. Exports are measured by the *gross* volume of steel (in ingot equivalent) shipped abroad. *Net* exports (i.e. gross exports less imports) is a more sophisticated measure but this has the drawback for our purposes that countries may be very successful in exporting a narrow or specialist line of products and yet achieve a trade deficit, and hence a negative performance rating, because they import quantities of products in which they have a temporary or longer-term capacity shortfall or some other relative disadvantage. Together with differences in freight costs and tariffs in a heterogeneous trading area, this factor also inhibits the adoption of a bilateral trade advantage analysis such as that employed by Owen[2] for certain EEC countries.

In strict theory, since we are proposing a causal relationship flowing *from* efficiency *to* export performance (an alternative hypothesis operating in the opposite direction can be formulated), we should consider export performance in the period immediately following the efficiency measure. This is a simple matter for the mid-1950s analysis, where to remove the effect of cyclical variations we have taken the average export share for the four years from 1955. But for the late-1960s analysis, our efficiency ratings refer to about 1968, and the latest date for which export data were available at the time of the calculations was 1969. Therefore we have taken the average for the four years to 1969. This removes most of the cyclical effect, but it does mean that some of the export performance results *precede* the data of the efficiency ratings. However, given the likelihood that most of our efficiency measures are subject to fairly severe errors, this is probably of little consequence.

(b) Late-1960s Structure and Subsequent Export Performance

The approach for this part of the enquiry was to conduct a multivariate linear regression analysis in which each country's export share is regressed upon several structural variables which might systematically explain observed differences in trade performance. We review the selected variables in turn, beginning with the dependent performance indicator.

This is the average annual share of each country's exports in the combined export of the nine nations of the enquiry for the four years commencing 1966 (EXSHARE). The indicator is to be preferred to the share of each country in total world trade, which is affected by the rising exports from producing countries not included in the enquiry.

The first independent variable, PLANTEFF, is the percentage of total reckonable capacity in each country contained in plants of 2.5 million tons capacity or above.

---

1 We implicitly assume, therefore, that the more efficient steel industries have a comparative advantage as well as an absolute advantage: this is probably not too unreasonable an assumption.

2 Nicholas Owen, op. cit., 1973.

These data are obtained from column 3 of Table 43. The results inadequately reflect the differential achievement of technical economies of scale in each country, because the prevailing m.e.s. is considerably in excess of the minimum scale adopted as efficient (see VIII (b)). Thus the larger is the average capacity of the plants classified as efficient, the higher will be the (adjusted) efficiency rating of the country concerned. However, our failure to take account of this is probably not so serious as appears at first sight, because inspection of our data suggests that in general, the countries with the highest (unadjusted) efficiency ratings also tend to have a larger average size of plant. Our expectation is that this variable will correlate positively with export performance, and if plant-related economies are an important explanatory element, the connection should be close.

The next variable is FIRMEFF, which is the percentage of adjusted capacity in companies with capacities of 2.5 million tons or above. Column 3 of Table 44 presents these data. Again there is the problem that the efficiency ratings do not adequately reflect the advantages which probably attach to the countries with the larger average firm sizes. It is to be expected that this variable will correlate significantly and positively with the dependent variable, but to a lesser degree than PLANTEFF, since the main economies of scale appear to be associated chiefly with plant size, and in most countries there is a shortfall, which is sometimes substantial, between the apparent efficiency level when firm sizes are considered and the measured level when plants are considered (see Table 45).

Next we consider inter-country differences in the size of the domestic market. This is indicated by the average annual apparent consumption of steel in ingot equivalent terms for the period 1966 to 1969 inclusive (DOMCON). Apparent consumption is defined as production *minus* exports *plus* imports, and the averaging process reduces the effect of cyclical fluctuations. It is possible that plant and firm size is to some degree dependent upon the size of the home market, and thus the variable may correlate positively with the dependent variable, and also with the plant and firm efficiency measures. On the other hand, the smaller the domestic market the greater may be the export drive to achieve as many of the scale-related benefits as possible.

We indicated in VII (b) above that differences in factor prices were likely to result in unit cost differences between the countries of the sample. Clearly, all else equal, the countries with relatively low costs may be expected to perform relatively well in export markets. To attempt to gauge the effect of this we have included as a variable an index of unit costs for modern integrated plants of m.e.s. (= 8 million tons) in each country producing hot-rolled strip. This is derived from Table 41 and is termed UNCOST. Since costs in the lowest-cost country (Italy) are taken as base, we would anticipate a negative relationship with the dependent variable; that is, the higher the relative costs, the poorer the export performance.

Finally we need to take account of inter-country differences in product-mix, since export performance may be related to the types of product available. To indicate this we have taken the percentage shares of flat-rolled products in total finished steel output for each country in 1968 (Canada 1967). This variable is termed PRODMIX. We cannot forecast its likely sign from *a priori* reasoning.

No account is taken in the analysis of the roles of tariffs, freight costs, prices, or exchange rates in determining export performance. This is both because the preparation of such data is a lengthy and complex procedure and also, more important because our objective is to assess the contribution of international structural differences to export performance variations, rather than to identify the principal determinants of export performance.

To summarise, we propose the following variables, the values of which are displa in Appendix 5. With the exception of variable 6, all steel volume measures are in ingot equivalent terms. There is one dependent variable.

1. EXSHARE : Percentage of combined aggregated exports of all the sample countries formed by the aggregated exports of each, 1966–1969 inclusive.

The independent variables are:

2. PLANTEFF : Percentage of total adjusted capacity contained in plants of 2.5 million tons capacity and above, *circa* 1968.

3. FIRMEFF : Percentage of total adjusted capacity contained in companies of 2.5 million tons capacity and above, *circa* 1968.

4. DOMCON : Average apparent consumption of steel in million tons, 1966–1969 inclusive.

5. UNCOST : Index of estimated unit costs in a modern integrated steelworks of 8 million tons crude steel capacity producing hot-rolled strip (Italy = 100).

6. PRODMIX : Percentage of total production of finished steel formed by flat-rolled products, 1968 (Canada 1967).

As a preliminary step, the simple correlation coefficients between all the variable were calculated, and the results are presented in Appendix 6. With a total of six sets of observations, a correlation coefficient of 0.7067 or above is necessary for the relationship between any two variables to be taken as differing significantly from zero. The inter-correlation between the independent variables is generally low and insignificant in all cases except for PLANTEFF and PRODMIX (0.874). Thus the proportion of flat-rolled products in total output is a fairly good proxy for the percentage of adjusted capacity in plants of 2.5 million tons or above. This is not unexpected, since we indicated in VII (d) that larger plants were required for the production of flat-rolled products than for other classes of products.

The correlation coefficients between the independent variables and the dependen variable are shown in Table 46. None are significantly different from zero at the 5 per cent level. PLANTEFF, which is our main indicator of scale-related efficiency, shows a slight negative correlation with EXSHARE, which is contrary to our expectation and indicates that the proportion of capacity in large plants (as defined) is unimportant in export performance. FIRMEFF shows virtually no relationship with the dependent variable, again failing to confirm the predicted direction of association. A similar outcome results when DOMCON is considered. UNCOST relates negatively and moderately with EXSHARE, confirming the prediction that lower factor costs promote export success. PRODMIX also shows a moderate negative relationship, indicating a tendency for those countries in which light and heavy rolled goods feature prominently to have relatively larger shares in exports.

Table 46 *Coefficients of Correlation between Export Performance and Structure Variables, Steel*

Independent Variables	Dependent Variable EXSHARE Correlation Coefficient
PLANTEFF	−0.3496
FIRMEFF	−0.1189
DOMCON	−0.0650
UNCOST	−0.4678
PRODMIX	−0.5007

The disappointingly low connection between the dependent variable and the principal indicators of the scale of production prevent us from claiming that inter-country variations in the proportion of capacity contained in large plants and firms contributed significantly to export performance in the late-1960s. However, tariffs, freight charges and other factors are likely to have distorted the pattern of trade, and we might perhaps hope for closer relationships in a dynamic analysis — that is, one which considers changes both in efficiency levels and in export performances.

(c) Structural Change and Performance, mid-1950s to late-1960s

To examine the effect of the changes in the structure of the industries upon their performance we conducted a less complex analysis in which the percentage changes in export performance between the two dates were regressed upon the percentage changes in plant efficiency during the period. A closer positive connection between changes in export performance and those in plant efficiency during a period may be expected than between the absolute levels of each at any point in time. One reason for this is that various external factors, among them tariff barriers and freight costs, undoubtedly play important roles in determining the pattern of trade flows at any point in time and may distort the contribution of plant efficiency. For example, *ceteris paribus,* high tariff protection by one country, or a group of countries, seems likely to reduce the shares in total exports (EXSHARE). However, if the barriers remain more or less constant relative to each other during time, changes in efficiency are likely to induce changes in export performance.[1] A second factor is that changes in the proportion of reckonable capacity in efficient plants may reflect more appropriately the rate of incorporation of technical progress through the employment of best-practice technology. This feature is not readily indicated by a consideration of the proportion of reckonable capacity in efficient plants at any point in time because some nations have developed large facilities through piecemeal expansion and which incorporate equipment of varying vintages.

Paralleling the analysis in sub-section (b) above, our dependent variable is ΔEXSHARE, the percentage points change in each country's share of the combined exports of the countries in the sample between the two dates, expressed as a percentage of the share in the mid-1950s. We expect that this will correlate positively with changes in efficiency, since international competition between countries is

---

1 This assumption is made in the following analysis but it is recognised to be heroic, given the staged tariff reductions of the E.E.C. nations.

likely to be sensitive to changes in their relative efficiencies.

Only one independent variable is employed, ΔPLANTEFF. This is the percentage points change in the proportion of reckonable capacity in "efficient" plants in each country between the two periods, expressed as a percentage of the proportion in the mid-1950s. The basic data for this variable are given in Table 43. Our reason for using the *percentage* changes in export performance and plant efficiency, as opposed to the *percentage point* changes is that the former weights given percentage point changes more heavily when they relate to a small export performance or plant efficiency level than when they refer to a larger base. This is desirable since, *a priori*, percentage point increases on a small base are more significant. The values of the variables are displayed in Appendix 7.

For the analysis, the following equation was tested:

$$Y_1 = a + bX_1 \qquad\qquad (1)$$

where

$$X_1 = \Delta\text{PLANTEFF}$$

$$Y_1 = \Delta\text{EXSHARE}$$

and the lower case letters are constants.

The results are as follows:

$$Y_1 = 53.61^* + 2.31X_1^* \qquad R^2 = 0.81 \qquad\qquad (2)$$
$$\quad (21.34) \quad (0.46)$$

The asterisks mark the constants which are significant at the five per cent level. The values of both constants are significant at the five per cent level, and the high R^2 shows that over 80 per cent of the variation in ΔEXSHARE can be attributed to ΔPLANTEFF. The equation indicates that a one per cent change in the share in total exports by any country (Y_1) requires an increase in the proportion of capacity in efficient plants (X_1) of 2.31 per cent.

This important result deserves some further comment. The regression analysis shows a strong and significant relationship between the rate of increase of the proportion of reckonable capacity in plants of efficient scale (Δ PLANTEFF) and the rate of increase of export share (Δ EXSHARE). The five countries in which ΔPLANTEFF increased during the period of the analysis are, in descending order of increase, Japan, Italy, Canada, the US. and the Netherlands (Appendix 7). On the basis of the latest available data (Table 42), the countries are also among the six nations with the highest proportions of BOS capacity in facilities of efficient scale (2.0 million tons and above). Hence ΔPLANTEFF seems a reasonable proxy for the relative up-to-dateness of technology in the countries of the enquiry.

The effect of technical progress is to raise the output rates from given inputs of productive factors, or in other words to move particular isoquants towards the origin and, depending on the nature of the technical progress, to alter their shapes. It follows that, given constant factor prices, as productivity rises so the scale curve (= long run average cost curve) shifts downwards, at least over part of its length. As a consequence unit costs at given scales of output with new technology will be lower than with the older methods. Further, depending on the relative positions and shapes of the scale curves, relatively smaller plants embodying best-practice

106

techniques will yield lower unit costs than larger plants of an older vintage. Thus we might expect the rate of incorporation of best-practice technology to offer some explanation of relative export performance – and this is indeed the case.

However, as we have shown, the m.e.s. associated with the BOS route for steel-making (i.e. the most modern route) is very large, and thus the acquisition of the benefits of modern technology requires also the construction of large scale plants. The contribution of the scale economies in best-practice plants to export perform-ance in the earlier regression analysis (sub-section (b) above) appears to be over-shadowed by the presence in several of the countries of relatively large plants of older vintage.

One further implication is that for successful competition internationally, nations need to ensure that technical progress is incorporated rapidly. In some cases the appropriate rationalisation strategy may be to encourage existing companies to build new facilities, even of sub-optimal size, rather than to embark first on extensive mergers which yield optimally-sized plants only after a considerable delay.

As our analysis has shown, 'efficiency' as measured by export performance seems to be closely related to the introduction of modern technology. But modern technology implies very large scale – much larger scale than previous technology. Thus the benefits of modern technology can only be fully grasped in conjunction with plants of very large scale.

X

Conclusions and Implications

(a) The results of the enquiry

The findings of our investigation can be summarised as follows:

(1) The steel industries considered differ widely in respect of their size, rate of growth of output, importance of foreign trade, investment rates, and productivity levels.

(2) In the costs of production of finished steel products, purchases of raw materials and supplies form well over one-half of the total, with wages and salaries accounting for about one-quarter. The basic oxygen system (BOS) yields the lowest unit cost for the production of crude steel in integrated steelworks having a supply of hot pig iron. Published data indicate considerable differences between the countries of the sample in the level of total unit costs. Raw material prices do not appear to differ greatly between the nations, but unit labour costs show considerable variation. This is due to differences in both productivity levels and wage rates. Countries outside North America — with the exception of the UK — succeed in achieving relatively low unit labour expenses mainly through lower earnings rates. The recent tendency has been for the differential between the unit labour costs of the European countries and those of North America to narrow. There is some suggestion of inter-country differences in capital costs, but we are unable to show the importance of these.

(3) The average sizes of the larger plants and firms differ considerably between the countries, with the US and Japan having the largest units. In all countries the trend in post-war years has been towards an increase in the average sizes of both plants and firms, accompanied by a growing share of total capacity contributed by the biggest units. In large part this has been achieved in North America and Japan through wholesale new construction, possibly affected in the North American case by anti-trust legislation preventing mergers, and prompted in the Japanese case by the high overall growth rate of the economy. In Europe (including the UK) developments have centred largely on mergers between producers, which have often been Government-aided, followed by efforts at rationalisation and modernisation mainly within the existing plant structures.

(4) Economies of scale in steel production flow mainly from savings in the costs of direct labour and capital, and are very strongly associated with the overall scale of individual plants. Company size is a less important factor. Some benefits also result from product specialisation and long production runs. Currently, the minimum efficient scale (m.e.s.) of an integrated plant producing steel by the BOS route and rolling a fairly comprehensive range of products is of the order of 8

million tons annually, while the comparable output level for a firm is about 12 million tons. Factor price differences between the countries do not significantly affect the slope of the scale curve over the output ranges in which the m.e.s. of the plant lies, but they do influence its position. However, with the exception of the US, UK and Canada, factor price variations do not cause unit costs to differ markedly between the nations at the plant m.e.s.

(5) Since most scale economies appear to be associated with the size of the plant, the broad ordering of the nations in terms of the extent to which they achieve the available economies of scale is indicated by Table 43 which sets out the proportion of total capacity contained in fairly efficient plants in each country. While the plant structures are clearly inadequate in most countries, the shares of total capacity contained in firms which are of a sufficient scale to operate plants of m.e.s. or above is without exception very high; hence plant-level rationalisation is the over-riding requirement in most industries. The efficiencies of the industries are also influenced by the degree of product specialisation they achieve at plant and firm level, but this seems unlikely to affect greatly the rankings of the nations as shown in the table. Although there is little overall connection between the efficiency ratings of the industries and their rates of output growth, labour productivity, investment and profitability, it is noticeable that the nations which score very low efficiency ratings — in particular France, Belgium-Luxembourg and the UK — also have poor achievements in each of the performance indicators.

(6) A particular feature of the development of the steel industry in the post-war period has been the speed of technical progress, associated chiefly with the introduction and continual improvement of the BOS. The m.e.s. of integrated steelworks has accordingly advanced rapidly — from around 2 million tons in the mid-1950s to over 8 million tons at the present time. None of the nations has been able to keep up with this rate of development; at the time of our study none of them had BOS installations of efficient scale in operation, and only three had plants with capacities in excess of 6 million tons. At the same time, increased supplies of scrap and cheaper electricity have made small-scale steelmaking in electric arc furnaces a viable proposition in certain localities, and the combined effect of these two developments has been to put pressure on medium-sized plants and firms.

(7) Differences between the nations in the proportions of total capacity contained in fairly efficient plants in the late-1960s do not explain the subsequent shares in exports of the countries. However, there is a close and significant connection between the rate of change of the proportion of capacity in efficient units between the mid-1950s and the late-1960s and the rate of change of export shares over the same period. This can be taken to indicate the contribution of the introduction of best-practice technology to international competitiveness.

Each country has recognised the necessity of improving the structure of its steel industry to allow the wider achievement of economies. It is worth considering what light our findings throw first upon the factors which limit the attainment of scale economies, and second upon the methods by which structural improvements can be made.

(b) Factors limiting the achievement of Economies of Scale

We can consider three main factors which may be suspected of inhibiting — to different extents in the various countries — the achievement of economies of scale. They are market size, the rate of growth of output, and the level of investment. In addition we may refer briefly to Government social and regional policies.

Considering first the size of the domestic market, the greater is the m.e.s. of plant or firm in relation to it, the smaller will be the number of optimally-sized units which can be supported, assuming there to be no opportunity for export sales. We suggested in Section VII that for integrated plants and firms producing steel via the BOS route and manufacturing a fairly wide range of hot-rolled products the respective minimum efficient scales were 8 and 12 million tons; these values are clearly very large both in absolute terms and relative to the domestic markets of the countries in the enquiry. In Table 47 the ratios of the plant and firm minimum efficient scales to the apparent crude steel consumption levels in each country in 1968 are shown; the ratios indicate the maximum number of plants and firms of efficient scale which could exist. For comparison we also show the actual numbers of plants and firms in operation.

It is immediately apparent that with the exception of the very large markets of the US and Japan, the numbers of plants and firms of efficient scale which could be supported in each country is very low — in some cases the market is too small to support even a single efficient unit. By contrast the numbers of plants and firms which actually exist are substantially greater than the ratios. To some extent this is because in each country small units (frequently using electric arc furnaces) serving specialist or localised markets can survive, and because (particularly in Belgium-Luxembourg, the Netherlands and Japan) exports permit the scale of output of the industry to exceed the size of the domestic market. But, as we have seen, in the majority of cases the excess of the actual numbers of plants and firms over the ratios results from the presence of sub-optimal units.

Table 47 *Steelmaking Plants and Firms: Actual Numbers in Operation and Theoretical Maxima if Each of Minimum Efficient Scale, by Country, 1968*

Country	Apparent Consumption ('000 tons)	Plants		Firms	
		Actual	Theoretical	Actual	Theoretical
Belgium-Luxembourg	4,049	18	0.5	10	0.3
France	18,045	48	2.3	26	1.5
Germany, F.R.	34,963	36	4.4	25	2.9
Italy	17,302	32	2.2	26	1.4
Netherlands	4,340	3	0.5	3	0.4
U.K.	23,115	70	2.9	27	1.9
U.S.	137,452	142	17.2	91	11.5
Canada	9,786	18	1.2	17	0.8
Japan	50,174	55	6.3	26	4.2

Source: B.S.C. *Statistical Handbook 1969,* and H.G. and G. Cordero, (eds.), op. cit., 1969.

For the majority of countries, therefore, rationalisation policies imply very high levels of concentration at firm level, and some may prefer to forego some of the benefits of increased efficiency in order to maintain a greater pressure of competition Alternatively, most nations would probably recognise the necessity for a policing agency to ensure that monopoly powers were not exerted to an unacceptable degree.

110

A second factor influencing the achievement of economies of scale is the growth of industry output. For two industries of equal size at a given point in time, the one with the faster subsequent rate of growth will be able to add facilities of optimal scale more frequently, and will expand more rapidly the proportion of its total output which is produced in efficient units. Where industries are of different sizes at the beginning of a period of expansion, their initial scales become relevant as well as their rates of growth. To illustrate, consider an industry in which the plant m.e.s. is 50 units of product. Any industry which adds 50 units of output annually can thus construct one optimal plant each year. If the industry's output (and capacity) at the start of the year is 500 units, output needs to grow by 10 per cent during the year to allow one optimal plant to be constructed and fully utilised. If, however, the initial output (and capacity) is 1000 units, output need grow by only 5 per cent for the same result. What this indicates is that given common technological conditions industries which are *absolutely* larger than others can afford to grow at slower *rates* and still construct efficient facilities at the same frequency. They will not, of course, achieve a comparable increase in the proportion of output coming from modern plants.

We indicated in Table 1 above that for most of the countries of the enquiry the general tendency in the post-war period has been for the annual quantity increase in output to be less than the present plant m.e.s. Under these conditions, countries are faced with a choice between, or some combination of, three possibilities. One is to build plants of optimal scale, but less frequently than countries in which the annual quantity increase in output is greater. If expansion lags behind demand, imports are absorbed to fill the gap, and once established these may be difficult to dislodge even when the domestic industry has the necessary production capability. A second response is to build at the same rate, but to construct plants of less-than-efficient scale; clearly the penalty here is the loss of economies of scale, a disadvantage which becomes increasingly severe as the size of plant is reduced. The third option is the expansion of existing plants. This has the advantages that small increments of capacity can be provided by adding individual units of equipment, and that frequently provision for expansion is incorporated in plants when they are first designed and built, so that expansion costs are reduced through the use of existing buildings and services. On the other hand, piecemeal additions to plants imply units of sub-optimal capacity, with the consequent loss of economies of scale. The argument so far unrealistically assumes that industries have no margin of spare capacity; in fact most do, and those with small quantity increases in demand may do no new net construction, a consequence which hampers increases in efficiency even more.

An additional benefit flowing from growth is that the cost of the replacement of existing capacity can be reduced. Under conditions of increasing returns to scale, additional capacity for replacement can be incorporated in new plants more cheaply than if units in existing plants are replaced — even with units which incorporate modern technology.

The influence of growth is qualified by the extent of cyclical variations in the demand for steel. Even though the trend increase in demand may be sufficient to induce producers to construct optimal facilities, marked demand fluctuations may lead to their building smaller plants in order to avoid periods of excessive surplus

111

capacity. Such variations may also encourage the retention of small plants to cater for peaks in demand. We have noted above that cyclical fluctuations have been particularly severe in the European countries in recent years, and almost certainly have been a contributory factor to their overall low levels of efficiency.

A further qualification of the effect of growth is the number and size-distribution of the principal producers. If they are each of approximately the same size, and if each has more or less the same degree of competitive power in the market, the total increases in demand will tend to be distributed between them in equal amounts. In these conditions the tendency will be for each to increase its productive capacity, and the greater the number of firms and the smaller the total amount of the increase in demand, the smaller will be each additional unit of capacity. Unless the overall increase in demand is very large, therefore, firms will tend to build plants of sub-optimal scale. The problem is exacerbated if the combined expectations of the producers regarding future increases in demand exceed the actual increases, for in that situation the industry will develop surplus capacity.

The fragmentation of additional demand between producers may prompt concentration-increasing mergers between them, or may lead to Government intervention, either through the provision and direction of investment, or through outright nationalisation. Our enquiry has shown that these have been typical responses within the European industries, including that of the UK, and there have been signs of their development also in Japan in recent years. An alternative solution to the problem of the dispersion of demand is for producers to agree to take it in turns to increase capacity, thus ensuring the construction of efficient units; however, this requires a high degree of mutual cooperation and trust between firms which may be difficult to obtain, particularly in periods of recession, and may contravene anti-monopoly regulations in several countries.

The third major factor affecting the attainment of economies of scale is the level of investment. In the private sector this is chiefly a function of the level of profits, which determines both the quantity of funds available from within the firm for reinvestment, and the amount of outside borrowing which is possible. In most of the steel industries of our enquiry, these sources have been supplemented by Government aid, given directly or indirectly. The review of investment trends in Section III showed wide differences between the countries in their rates of investment expenditure per ton of annual output, with expenditure generally being highest in those industries which were subsequently shown to have the largest proportions of total capacity in fairly efficient plants. However, profits during the 1960s were in general insufficient to support the levels of investment required to increase plant and firm sizes to take full advantage of the economies of scale released by the sharp upward increase in the m.e.s. In part this was due to the depressed trading conditions, which combined with some new net investment produced surplus capacity and raised unit production costs and in part also to Government price regulation in several countries. A measure of the investment shortfall was given in a recent report for the Commission of the European Communities. It was estimated that a modern integrated steelworks to produce plate via the BOS route with an annual crude steel output of 7 to 8 million tons would cost about $16 billion to construct. This is more than three times the combined cash flow of the eight largest producers in the EEC in 1968.[1]

A final point which inhibits structural improvements is Government social and regional policies which may lead to the continuance of obsolete, sub-optimal plants in order to maintain employment opportunities and to the inefficient division of investment between plants and regions. As we have noted, these features have been most pronounced in the European industries.

(c) Policies for Increased Efficiency

There are three chief ways in which the steel industries of the countries of this enquiry may increase the degree to which they achieve the available economies of scale: increases in firm size, increases in plant size, and increases in the degree of product specialisation in both plants and firms.

Table 17 above showed that in the late-1960s, the average sizes of the larger firms and plants were, in most countries, considerably below the output level at which economies of scale are fully attained. The only two exceptions are the large firm sizes in the US and Japan. Hence there is generally scope for improvements in efficiency by raising both firm and plant sizes. However, the analysis in VIII (b) and (c) showed that this need is most pressing for plants. Whereas the percentages of total reckonable capacity in firms capable of supporting a single plant of m.e.s. or above are consistently high in each country, the corresponding percentages for plants show extensive variation. This suggests that in most of the countries it is the small scale of plant rather than the small scale of firm which causes a marked loss of potential economies of scale; our finding that most of the available economies are associated with the size of the plant rather than with the size of the firm underline the significance of this.

Our enquiries also suggest that those countries with relatively small scale plants and firms could overcome this disadvantage to some extent by increasing the degree of product specialisation. In general the range of products produced by plants and firms is broadly the same in each country, but the larger plant and firm sizes in the US and Japan imply that the length of production runs in those countries is proportionately longer than elsewhere. Thus to some degree the other nations could profit by reducing their product ranges within the industry as a whole, within the firm and within the plant. However, there are substantial difficulties in the way of this kind of development. Commercial prudence requires that industries, firms, and to a lesser extent plants, produce several classes of product, since the cyclical fluctuations for each category differ both in timing and amplitude. Further, rolling mills are generally highly specific and there are severe limits to the ranges of products which can be processed. To take an extreme example, it is not possible to use bar mills to roll strip.

The improvements in the three dimensions of scale could be achieved by one or more of three methods: horizontal mergers between producers, increased co-operation between producers, and direct Government intervention. In recent years mergers have been important in reshaping the steel industries of all but one of the European countries of the enquiry. The exception is the Netherlands, where a single producer has dominated the industry during the entire post-war period.

1 Commission des Communautés Européennes, op. cit., 1971, p. 161.

In three of the countries, the national Government and/or the Commission of the European Communities has been instrumental in promoting at least some of the rationalisation. The most extensive Government involvement has, of course, been in the UK where virtually the entire iron and crude steel capacity, together with a high proportion of rolling capacity was nationalised in 1967. In France the Government has provided low interest funds to promote mergers and aid rationalisation. In Italy the European Bank for Investment has played an important role in merger developments in the steel industry. Mergers have only very recently been an important feature of structural change in Japan, where the two major producers combined in 1970. In the US and Canada mergers have been virtually ruled out by anti-trust legislation.

The main benefits resulting from the most important mergers have been reviewed in Section VI. The immediate increase in firm size allows fairly early consolidation of research and development and marketing activity together with improvements in the distribution system. Later a more efficient allocation of production between plants may be possible. This can be achieved both by concentrating the production of certain products on particular plants, and by transferring production from small, obsolete units to larger plants with spare capacity. However, the main plant-level economies can only be achieved when additional investment allows new production facilities of optimal scale to be constructed and existing plants to be expanded. The merger may assist in this respect by concentrating a given amount of investment upon fewer, larger plants than would have been the case in the absence of the amalgamation, but the impetus to additional investment is severely limited unless the merged firm is able to generate more investment than its previously separate component firms. This can occur only if (a) the merged firm becomes more efficient and generates greater profits; (b) the merged firm exercises greater monopoly power in the market, again generating additional profits, or (c) the greater size of the merged firm allows it to raise more external finance and/or to raise it more cheaply. While the latter is likely to be of some significance, especially where the rationalisation is Government-induced, (b) is unlikely to have much effect during periods in which demand is depressed or price is subject to control, and (a) may be difficult to achieve until after the plant structure has been rationalised. In situations where mergers are sanctioned and promoted by Governments, there is a pressing need to provide adequate finance not only for the rationalisation of the firm structure but also for that of the plant: and ideally to ensure that the expected benefits are actually achieved after the merger, without undue impairment of the competitive environment.

The difficulties of improving efficiency by merger raises the question of whether an alternative course is preferable. One way is to allow the more successful producers to expand at the expense of the others, but without being permitted to take them over or to purchase their assets. Broadly this has been the pattern of development in the US under (chiefly) Section 7 of the Clayton Act. The long-term advantage of this approach is that it forces firms to plan ahead and to construct new facilities rather than be tempted to purchase existing firms in order to obtain immediate expansion of their productive capacity. The policy has its greatest attraction when the annual additions to demand are large enough to allow the

114

expanding producers to add additional facilities of approximately minimum efficient scale. Among the disadvantages are that even the more efficient producers may be unable to raise sufficient capital for large-scale new investment, especially in periods of recession, and that the efficiency of the domestic industry may be impaired and its growth hampered, causing costs and prices to rise and imports to take a rising share of consumption. Further, market forces are seldom strong enough to cause sub-optimal and inefficient firms to leave an industry immediately, and consequently production may be characterised by extensive surplus capacity for a considerable period, leading possibly to aggressive and mutually damaging pricing policies.

An alternative to increased competition between producers is increased cooperation. In the short-term this could permit increased product specialisation, allowing longer runs and the eradication of much surplus capacity. In the longer-term, additional capacity could be allocated among the producers to ensure the construction of optimally-sized units by the most suitable firms, and to reduce the destabilising effect of sudden additions of large increments of capacity which modern technology requires. Such developments require a great degree of mutual trust between producers, and it seems likely that the vagaries of the steel industry, particularly the substantial cyclical fluctuations in demand, are likely to prevent, more or less effectively, the emergence of such a level of confidence. Prior to nationalisation, the major producers in the UK steel industry attempted through the Iron and Steel Federation to promote joint rationalisation plans, but were hampered in this by the natural desires of each of the producers to manufacture a wide enough range of goods to insulate them against the demand fluctuations for each product-class, and by the restraints on cooperation imposed on them by the restrictive practices legislation.[1] Rather more success appears to have been achieved in the West German industry through the formation of sales and production planning syndicates.

Underlying each of these courses of action is the need to increase investment. We indicated above that this fell short of the required level in most countries. The absolutely large amounts of capacity required for modern efficient plants mean that chronic overcapacity is a feature of most steel industries, and the importance of the steel industry in the respective national economies renders it peculiarly vulnerable to price control. Both of these elements are suggestive of eventual inadequate investment and imply the need for Government aid. This has occurred to the greatest extent in France and Italy, where it has undoubtedly assisted rationalisation and the construction of up-to-date plants.

The above discussion suggests that for the long-term efficiency of the steel industry a policy of competition without the ability to merge is perhaps the most appropriate, provided that the trend annual quantity additions to output are large, and close to the prevailing plant m.e.s. In the absence of these conditions, merger, supplemented by Government finance for investment, is perhaps the second-best alternative, but supervision of developments is essential, especially to ensure rationalisation.

1 cf. Development Coordinating Committee, op. cit., p. 9.

Appendix 1

The Manufacture of
Finished Steel Products

I. Introduction

In this appendix, the processes involved in the manufacture of steel products are briefly described.[1] Steel can be defined as an alloy of pure iron with less than two per cent carbon by weight.[2] Two qualities of steel are customarily distinguished: *common* and *special*. In the UK, the first refers to steel containing less than 0.6 per cent carbon by weight. Special steel includes that containing alloys (such as molybdenum, tungsten, vanadium, chromium, nickel, and manganese) above specified minimum proportions by weight. These alloys provide particular characteristics affecting amongst other features the mechanical, physical and corrosion-resistance properties of the steel. There are two important sub-divisions. *Stainless* and *heat-resisting steels*, which respectively do not readily discolour and withstand high temperatures, contain relatively high proportions of chromium. *High-speed* and *tool steels* contain tungsten and vanadium and are used for a variety of cutting operations. Special steels also include high-carbon steels, which contain at least 0.6 per cent carbon by weight, and only very small traces of the impurities phosphorus and sulphur. Often, high-carbon steels also contain alloys. The several classes of steel described are generally distinguished in each of the countries covered by the present enquiry, although the precise definitions differ between them.

II. Raw Materials

Steel is made from pig iron, from scrap, or from a combination of both, together with various oxides, fluxes and finishings. In the countries studied, the importance of scrap as a raw material for steel manufacture has increased considerably in recent years, and most countries have some steel-producing facilities which are based entirely upon scrap.

Pig iron is usually produced in a *blast furnace*. Iron-bearing materials such as ore, sinter (agglomerated ore dust and other fine particles), slag and iron or steel scrap are charged into the top of the furnace together with fuel (coke) and flux (usually limestone). Heated air is blown in at the bottom. This causes the coke to burn, producing heat to melt the iron, and carbon monoxide and other reactants to reduce the ore (i.e., remove the oxygen combined with the metal). The limestone

---

1   Full details of the various production processes are given in H.E. McGannon, (ed.), *The Making, Shaping and Treating of Steel*, United States Steel Corporation, 8th ed. 1964.

2   Ibid., p. 3.

116

forms a fluid slag with the impurities in the ore, which in turn regulates the sulphur content of the iron. Furnaces are in blast continuously for up to three or four years, and the molten iron is tapped every four to six hours, the frequency depending chiefly upon the quality of the ore being smelted. In a fully integrated works, the molten pig iron can be charged directly into the steel-making furnace. Otherwise, it is cast into moulds, and for subsequent steel-making is either re-heated or charged cold into the furnace. Scrap used in blast-furnaces is mostly that generated when the furnaces are tapped and the molten iron cast.[1]

III. Crude Steel Production

Crude, or *raw,* steel has not yet been rolled, and is usually in ingot form. It is produced in a furnace from hot or cold pig iron, or iron and steel scrap, or some combination of the two, through the oxidation of carbon and various impurities contained in the metal, such as silicon, sulphur, phosphorus and manganese. Special steels are produced through the addition of alloying substances to the furnaces. These contribute particular characteristics to the steel. Scrap is obtained from external sources and internally, principally from ingot and billet ends (which are always rejected because of deformation caused in cooling) and from metal sheared-off in the rolling-mills. Four methods of steel production are commonly employed at present, and they are considered briefly:—

(a) *Acid and Basic Bessemer Processes*

In both of these techniques, molten pig iron is charged into a vessel (together sometimes with a small quantity of cold scrap), and cold air is blown through the metal from the bottom. The heat generated through the oxydisation of the impurities is sufficient for the refining process to take place without externally-applied heat being necessary. The techniques require a supply of hot metal, and, because all the impurities cannot be removed, are used for the production of common grades of steel. The conversion process takes about fifteen minutes. The acid process was the first to be developed for the large-scale production of steel, and, because the converter is lined with acid refractories, can be used only for the reduction of iron with a low phosphorus content. Its importance in the world production of steel has declined relatively since 1880 and absolutely since 1910.[2] At present, it is often used in conjunction with open-hearth furnaces (see below) in the "duplex" process.

In the basic (Thomas) process, first patented in 1879, the converter is lined with basic refractories, allowing the reduction of high-phosphorus iron. It has declined in importance relatively since 1910,[3] and among the countries of our sample is most widely employed in France and Belgium-Luxembourg owing to the availability of the high-phosphorus ores of Lorraine.

1 Ibid., p. 387.

2 Economic Commission for Europe, *Comparison of Steel-Making Processes,* (New York: United Nations), 1962, Fig. 2, p. 2.

3 Ibid.

117

(b) Open Hearth Furnaces

This process is now technically obsolete, and in decreasing use. It was developed towards the end of last century, and offered several advantages over Bessemer. Heat is supplied externally instead of chiefly from the purifying reaction in the furnace, and this allows the temperature of the furnace and the speed of the reaction to be carefully controlled. The technique also allows the use of a high proportion of scrap, and of pig iron with an intermediate phosphorus content of between 0.035 and 0.075 per cent. Further, the yield of steel from a given charge of pig iron is much higher than with the Bessemer system.[1] The charge of metal into the furnace is usually of hot pig iron and cold scrap, although sometimes the entire charge is of cold metal. Accurate furnace control allows special as well as common steel to be produced. Against these advantages, however, the production of steel takes about eight hours, and unless several furnaces are in use simultaneously, the continuous flow of ingots necessary for subsequent processes cannot be maintained.[2]

(c) Electric Furnaces

These are of two main types. *Arc* furnaces heat the metal primarily through radiation by a current passed between two electrodes. In *induction* furnaces, a current is passed directly through the charge to melt it. The first type is used for the production of steel from largely unrefined metal; the second is used primarily for melting refined steel for alloying purposes. *Vacuum* furnaces, designed to produce steel with improved mechanical and physical properties, are in an early stage of development. Electric furnaces have the advantages that the melting process can be precisely controlled, and that a cold charge, composed entirely of scrap can be used. Hot pig iron is sometimes also used. It takes about six hours to refine a charge of metal.[3] Until recently electric furnaces were used chiefly for the production of special steels, but are now being more widely applied to common steel manufacture as the relative cost of electricity is reduced, and as scrap becomes a more important source of supply.

(d) Basic Oxygen Systems (BOS)

Steel refining in these techniques, which include the L-D, Kaldo and Rotor processes, involves the blowing of oxygen at high velocity onto the surface of the molten metal in a Bessemer-type converter. This combines with the impurities in the charge, and, depending upon the process employed, the reduction of the metal is completed in between one and two hours. The techniques have been developed since the early 1950s, the main process, the LD, being used chiefly for the refinement of low phosphorus iron. They have the advantages of simplicity and a high rate of output as a result both of the large vessel size which is possible,[4] and the short cycle time.

1   H.E. McGannon, (ed.), op. cit., pp. 28–9, 386.

2   C. Pratten and R.M. Dean, *The Economies of Large-Scale Production in British Industry,* University of Cambridge, Department of Applied Economics, Occasional Paper 3, (Cambridge: Cambridge University Press), 1965, p. 68.

3   H.E. McGannon, (ed.), op. cit., p. 534.

4   Up to 300 tons per heat. See United States Senate, Committee on Finance, *Steel Imports,* (Washington, D.C.: U.S. Government Printing Office), 1967, Table B-2, p. 274.

However, a supply of hot pig iron, forming about 70 per cent of the total charge, is required and the process can only be installed in integrated works having blast furnaces. So far, the processes have been employed for the production of the common grades of steel, because of the difficulty of controlling accurately the reaction in the furnace.

After refining, the liquid metal is tapped from the furnace into ladles, and poured either into large ingot moulds or, increasingly, into a *continuous casting* machine. Ingots are reheated in *soaking pits* to prepare them for subsequent hot working. In continuous casting, the metal is run into moulds of smaller cross-sectional dimensions than those of ingots, and continously withdrawn as it solidifies. For the production of rolled products, this process by-passes the stages of reheating and primary rolling (see below) necessary if ingots are cast.

IV. Finishing

The steel is now ready for forming and shaping into a variety of finished products. The first stage is *hot working,* which includes hot rolling and forging. In *hot rolling,* to which the majority of steel produced by the countries of our enquiry is subject, the metal is passed between series of horizontal rolls, arranged one above the other as in a mangle, until the required cross-section is obtained. If ingots are used, they must first be reduced to more manageable proportions in a *primary* (or cogging) mill. This reduces them to *blooms, billets,* or *slabs.* Blooms and billets are fairly square in cross-section, and are of considerable length. Typically, blooms have the greatest cross-sectional area.[1] Slabs have oblong cross-sections and tend to be of short length. The pieces are then passed through mills which roll them either into flat products (plate, sheet, strip, coil etc.) or into other products such as bars, angles, shapes, sections, rails, etc. For the latter, the rolls of the mills are grooved to produce the required shape. In *forging,* the metal is mechanically or hydraulically hammered or pressed into the form of the finished product.

Although a considerable proportion of rolling mill output can be dispatched to users without further processing, some requires additional rolling, and treatment. *Cold rolling* is applied to some flat products and bars and rods. It serves to reduce the metal to the required dimensions, where this cannot be achieved at the hot-rolling stage, to provide a smooth, dense surface, and to improve the mechanical properties of the metal (particularly its tensile strength). *Tubes* and *pipes* are produced by one of four principal methods. In *continuous welding,* the tube is formed from a hot metal strip, bent longitudinally, and the weld made by rolling one opposing edge over the other. This technique is used mainly for the production of general tubes. In *electric resistance welding,* (E.R.W.), the tube is formed from cold metal, and the opposing edges of the strip are fused by the passing of an electric current. A high-quality weld is obtained with this process. Both techniques can be used to produce tube of circular or rectangular cross-section. Seamless tubes are produced by *piercing,* in which a mandrel is passed through a billet. Large diameter pipes and tubes may be produced either by the E.R.W. process from very wide sheet, or by *spiralling* coil and welding the seam.

1   In the range $6'' \times 6''$ to $12'' \times 12''$ as compared with $2'' \times 2''$ to $5'' \times 5''$ for billets. See H.E. McGannon, (ed.), op. cit., p. 631.

Heat treatment is used to remove stress produced in steel through cooling and to enhance one or more of its properties (strength, hardness, ductility, wear-resistance, etc.). The process consists of fairly slowly heating the metal to, and maintaining it for a specified period at, the temperature at which the required structural changes take place. The metal is then either quenched in water or oil, or allowed to cool more slowly, depending upon the particular characteristic required. Such treatment is very important in the production of special steels. Sheet, strip and coil may be coated with another metal to increase corrosion resistance. Before coating, the metal is thoroughly cleaned, usually in an acid bath, a process known as *pickling*. The two most important coating processes are *tinning* and *galvanising*. Tinplate is produced either by dipping the steel in a bath of molten tin, or more usually, electrolytically in an acid bath. In galvanising, sheet steel is dipped into a bath of molten zinc.

Appendix 2 Cycles in the Production of Crude Steel by Country, 1950–69

Year	Belgium-Luxembourg	France	Germany, F.R.	Italy	Netherlands	E.E.C.	U.K.	U.S.	Canada	Japan
				Percentage change over previous year						
1951	+30.6	+17.9	+11.4	+29.7	+13.1	+17.5	−4.0	+8.5	+1.9	+42.5
1952	−0.8	+10.1	+17.0	+18.7	+23.6	+11.0	+5.0	−11.4	+3.8	+2.9
1953	−10.9	−7.4	−2.4	−1.0	+25.8	−5.2	+7.3	+19.8	+12.1	+11.2
1954	+8.9	+5.9	+12.1	+20.2	+7.8	+19.0	+5.2	−20.9	−22.4	+3.6
1955	+16.4	+17.3	+22.4	+28.2	+5.6	+20.0	+6.9	+32.5	+42.8	+22.7
1956	+7.5	+6.4	+8.7	+9.5	+7.1	+7.9	+4.4	−1.6	+16.6	+19.8
1957	−0.5	+4.5	+5.7	+14.8	+12.7	+5.4	+5.0	−2.2	−4.8	+14.6
1958	−3.8	+3.1	+7.0	−7.6	+21.4	−3.1	−9.8	−24.4	−13.6	−3.0
1959	+7.6	−5.8	+21.3	+7.8	+16.1	+9.0	+3.2	+9.6	+38.5	+73.9
1960	+11.6	+1.5	+23.4	+21.7	+16.3	+15.3	+20.4	+6.2	−1.6	+33.1
1961	−1.3	+1.7	−1.9	+10.9	+1.5	+0.6	−9.1	−1.3	+11.7	+27.7
1962	+2.2	−1.9	−2.7	+4.0	+5.9	−0.7	−7.2	+0.3	+10.6	−2.6
1963	+1.8	+1.8	−3.0	+4.1	+12.2	+0.3	+9.9	+11.1	+14.3	+14.4
1964	+15.0	+12.7	+18.2	−5.6	+13.0	+13.2	+16.5	+16.3	+11.4	+26.3
1965	+3.5	−0.9	−1.4	+29.5	+18.6	+3.8	+3.0	+3.5	+10.3	+3.4
1966	−3.2	−0.1	−4.1	+7.6	+3.8	−1.0	−10.0	+2.0	−0.4	+16.1
1967	+6.7	+0.4	+4.0	+16.5	+4.5	+5.6	−1.7	−5.1	−7.3	+30.1
1968	+15.6	+3.8	+12.0	+6.8	+9.0	+9.7	+8.2	+3.3	+19.7	+7.6
1969	+11.9	+10.3	+10.1	−3.2	+27.1	+8.8	+2.2	+7.5	−10.3	+22.8
Total Output 1969 (m. tons)	18.4	22.5	45.3	16.4	4.7	107.3	26.8	128.2	9.4	82.2

Source: B.S.C. *Statistical Handbook 1970.*

Appendix 3 Published Home Trade Steel Prices in the United Kingdom, E.E.C. and the U.S.A. May 1971[1]

	Rate of Exchange to £	Re-Rolled Billets Tested 4" 100 tons (of 2240 lbs) £	Plates 6' X 3' X .375" 50 tons £	Structural Plates 20' X 5' X 5" 25 tons £	Ship Plates Lloyds D 20' X 6' X 1" 10 tons £	Boiler Plates 20' X 6'3" X .375" 10 tons £	Heavy Angles 5" X 5" X .5" 25 tons £	Channels Structural 6" X 3" 10 tons £	Broad Flanged Beams and Columns Structural 24" X 9" 25 tons £	Re-Rolled Rounds Basis 1" dia. 25 tons £	Steel for Reinforcement 20 mm. dia. 50 tons £
United Kingdom		47.10	66.55	62.40	69.55	69.00	60.50	58.70	57.90	59.85	59.25
West Germany	DM 8.784	49.90	74.20	71.30	86.35[3]	86.35	61.30	—	—	59.55	56.10
Belgium	B. Frs. 120	51.10	66.55	69.95	82.00	79.90	59.60	64.05	—	58.35	55.10
France	N.Frs. 13.330	46.50	75.55	73.25	84.30	89.25	58.00	64.65	71.45	55.95	54.35
Luxembourg	B. Frs. 120	39.10	74.30	75.15	—	—	61.45	70.05	77.25	60.15	58.65
Italy	Lire 1500	42.80	68.80[2]	69.80	76.90	76.90	63.70	62.85	72.30	57.30	55.25
Netherlands	DG 8.688	—	61.50	63.80	75.75	76.45	—	—	—	59.95	52.25[2]
U.S.	$ 2.40	—	81.95	78.20	—	85.70	79.60	82.90	77.30	82.20	—

Re-Rolled Flats Basis 3" X .75"	Re-Rolled Angles Basis 2" X 2" X .25"	Wire Rods Soft Basic 6.5 mm dia.	Hot Rolled Strip Basis	Hot Rolled Coil Structural Basis 5' X .25"	Hot Rolled Coil Basis 3' X .099"	Cold Reduced Coil G.P. Quality	Cold Reduced Coil Edd Quality 4' X .039"	Galvanised Plain Coil 39" X .028"	Electrolytic Tinplate 8 oz over 29" X 23" X .0099"

	Rate of Exchange to £	25 tons	50 tons	25 tons	50 tons	50 tons	50 tons	100 tons	50 tons	25 tons	50 tons
		£	£	£	£	£	£	£	£	£	£
United Kingdom		60.25	62.40	60.65	66.55	59.10	60.45	68.50	75.75	91.95	13.300
West Germany	DM 8.784	62.45	61.90	58.60	61.70	67.85[2]	61.15	73.30[2]	83.15	105.70	13.968
Belgium	B. Frs. 120	60.45	59.65	56.40	59.00	70.00	55.25	76.10	79.05	90.60	14.321
France	N.Frs. 13.330	58.15	57.55	57.90	59.15	70.20[2]	59.50[2]	76.10	78.90	96.60	12.578
Luxembourg	B. Frs. 120	62.30	61.45	57.80	61.45	–	–	77.80	80.80	101.50	–
Italy	Lire 1500	58.65	60.00	57.30	59.65	66.75	58.65	73.55	81.65	91.85	14.265
Netherlands	DG 8.688	–	–	59.95	62.30	–	49.70	66.50	79.70	–	12.986
U.S.	$ 2.40	83.10	85.00	80.90	75.40	–	69.80	88.50	89.90	104.80	14.815

Notes: (1) (i) The table above is based on the published home trade prices ruling on 1st May, 1971 for representative steel products in the United Kingdom, E.E.C. and the U.S.A.

     (ii) For products other than tinplate, the prices shown are for a ton of 2,240 lbs. For tinplate, the prices are for a standard area of tinplate (S.A.T.) which is 100,000 sq. in. In all cases the price relates to orders of approximately the quantity shown.

     (iii) Except for tinplate BSC prices are delivered customers' works. The E.E.C. and U.S.A. prices, with the exception of tinplate, include an estimate for the average cost of carriage within the country of origin.

     (iv) The prices shown for E.E.C. countries do not include turnover or similar taxes, current rates of which are West Germany 11%; Belgium 18%; France 23%; Luxembourg 10%, Italy 4% and Netherlands 14%.

   (2) Temporary rebates operating in E.E.C. have been taken into consideration in calculating the prices above. The rebates cover the following products:–

       Germany – Hot Rolled Coil (.25″), Cold Reduced Coil (general purpose)
       Italy   – Plates (.375″)
       France   – Hot Rolled Coil
       Netherlands– Steel for Reinforcement

   (3) Three Sales Offices publish separate price lists for shipbuilding steel. Under these lists the price for Lloyds D is £82.30 per ton.

Source: British Steel Corporation.

Appendix 4

Method of Derivation of Crude Steel Capacity by Plant and Firm, mid-1950s and late-1960s

The estimates of plant and firm capacities used to prepare the size distributions for the mid-1950s and the late-1960s given in Section VI have been obtained from the appropriate editions of *Iron and Steel Works of the World*.[1] For some plants and firms — particularly in the US and Canada in the late-1960s, in the UK in the mid-1950s, and in France at both times — details are given only of the standing capacities of the individual steel furnaces, and it has been necessary to estimate their annual rates of capacity output. This has been done using material from an investigation by the Economic Commission for Europe of the United Nations[2] which shows the estimated ranges of annual productivity per ton of standing capacity of several types of steel-making installation producing low-carbon steels and using both low and high phosphorus pig iron.

To avoid undue overestimation the annual capacity estimates have been derived by taking the mid-point of the productivity range for each system when high phosphorus pig iron is used, which generally yields the lowest rate of output of crude steel. The relevant data are as follows:

Types of Installation	Annual Productivity per ton of Standing Capacity tons
Open Hearth	950
Electric Arc	2,500
Basic Bessemer (Thomas)	8,000
Basic Oxygen Systems: OLP; LD-AC; LD-Pompey	6,500
Kaldo	5,500
Rotor	4,500

Against this, however, the productivity estimates refer to the early 1960s, and because of a likely tendency for typical yields to improve through time, probably overestimate annual capacities in the mid-1950s and underestimate them in the late-1960s. The most important consequence of this for the relevant countries is an overestimation of the importance of large companies in the mid-1950s and an underestimation in the late-1960s.

1 H.G. and G. Cordero, (eds.), *Iron and Steel Works of the World*, (London: Metal Bulletin Books Ltd), 1957, 1969.

2 Economic Commission for Europe, *Comparison of Steelmaking Processes*, (New York: United Nations), 1962.

Appendix 5   Values of Variables for Structure/Performance Analysis for late-1960s, Steel

Country	EXSHARE	PLANTEFF	FIRMEFF	Variables DOMCON	UNCOST	PRODMIX
	%	%	%	m. tons	%	%
Belgium-Luxembourg	19.62	27.17	85.50	4.00	107.22	46.70
France	12.33	27.44	108.60	18.86	104.49	49.70
Germany, F.R.	23.27	52.67	73.00	32.80	105.88	55.80
Italy	4.13	42.67	72.20	16.89	100.00	50.90
Netherlands	4.84	100.00	100.00	4.40	102.08	78.20
U.K.	7.15	32.71	99.10	22.89	123.75	58.90
U.S.	4.82	81.52	89.30	133.38	126.15	66.80
Canada	2.12	90.31	90.30	9.81	127.03	64.60
Japan	21.71	76.33	99.10	50.14	102.41	57.90

Appendix 6

Correlation Matrix of Variables, Structure/ Performance Analysis for late-1960s, Steel

	Independent			Dependent		
Dependent	EXSHARE	PLANTEFF	FIRMEFF	DOMCON	UNCOST	PRODMIX
EXSHARE	–					
PLANTEFF	−0.3500	–				
FIRMEFF	−0.1189	0.0979	–			
DOMCON	−0.0650	0.2775	−0.0345	–		
UNCOST	−0.4678	0.2081	0.1092	0.4149	–	
PRODMIX	−0.5007	0.8743	0.2654	0.2209	0.2914	–

Appendix 7

Values of Variables for Analysis of Effect of Changes in Structure upon Changes in Performance, mid-1950s to late-1960s, Steel

Country	Variables	
	Δ EXSHARE %	Δ PLANTEFF %
Belgium-Luxembourg	−18.25	−29.92
France	−34.87	−57.95
Germany, F.R.	+16.58	n.a.
Italy	+27.86	+13.70
Netherlands	+77.94	+1.21
U.K.	−35.59	−59.87
U.S.	−64.92	+8.58
Canada	+64.34	+11.41
Japan	+330.75	+94.62

Source: Column 2, B.S.C. *Statistical Handbook, 1970;* Column 3, Table 43.

Index

Allegheny-Ludlum, 40, 57, 77
American Iron and Steel Institute, 36(n),
    59(n), 60, 65
Arbed, s.a., 40, 41

Bain, J.S., 3, 37, 67, 68, 88
Bank finance:
    importance in Japan, 66
Basic oxygen system, 118–9,
    costs of, 22–6
    development, 24, 26, 108
    economies of scale in, 70–2, 79–85, 109
    importance of, 15–18, 94
    in Japan, 63
    Kaldo process, 70, 118
    L.D. process, 70, 118–19
Belgium–Luxembourg:
    structure of steel industry, 39–42
Benson report, 22(n), 53(n), 54, 68, 69, 70,
    71, 72, 73, 74, 75, 77(n), 115(n)
Bessemer converters, 18, 70, 117
Bethlehem Steel Corp., 56, 57, 59
Blake, C., 9, 52(n), 88(n)
Blast furnaces, 69–70
    in iron production, 116–17
    size, 15
Board of Trade (see Department of Trade
    and Industry)
British Steel Corporation, 31(n), 47(n),
    50(n), 50–6, 60(n)
    formation, 51, 55
    merger benefits, 88
    revenue and costs, 21
    structure, 55
Brittan, S., 1(n)
Burn, D., 34, 49(n), 54(n), 92, 97

Canada:
    structure of steel industry, 60–2
Capital costs:
    international comparisons, 32, 34, 92
Cartwright, W.F., 25, 27(n)
Chambre Syndicale de la Sidérurgie
    Française, xiv, 42(n), 44(n)
Cockerill, A., 2(n), 78(n), 87(n)
Cockerill, s.a., 40, 41, 88
Comité de la Sidérurgie Belge, 39(n)
Commerce Clearing House, Inc., 59(n)
Commission of the European Communities,
    34(n), 45, 71, 72(n), 74, 75, 88,
    89(n), 113(n)
Competition:
    and efficiency, 113, 114–15
    legislation, 114

policy, 59, 65
Concentration, 2, 4–5, 50
Continuous casting, 20, 74, 119
Cooperation agreements, 45–6
    and economies of scale, 112, 113, 115
Cordero, H.G. and G., 37(n), 40(n), 47(n),
    52(n), 56(n), 57(n), 61(n), 124(n)
Cost-engineering technique, 78
Costs:
    and technology, 22–7
    and trade performance, 103–5
    as a performance indicator, 101
    capital, 32, 34–5
    employment, 31–2
    in B.S.C., 21–2
    International comparisons, 27–35, 108
Cyert, R.M., and George, K.D., 3(n)

Department of Commerce (U.S.), 58(n)
Department of Trade and Industry, 52(n),
    53(n), 55(n)
Development Coordinating Committee (see
    Benson report)
Discounted cash flow, 34–5
Dumping, 36, 60

Earnings, 31–2
Economic Commission for Europe, 39(n), 96,
    97(n), 117(n), 124(n)
Economic Commission for Latin America, 69,
    71, 73
Economic growth, 1–3, 111–12
Economies of scale, 108–9
    and investment, 112–13
    and market size, 110
    and output growth rates, 111
    and policies for increased efficiency,
    113–15
    definitions and sources, 67–8
    in companies, 85–9
    in plants, 77–85
    in iron-making, 69–70
    in rolling and finishing, 73–7
    in steel-making, 70–3
    measurement techniques, 78–9
Economist, The, 45(n), 46(n), 56(n), 66(n)
Efficiency, 109
    and trade performance, 101–7
    of processes, 93–5
    of steel companies, 98–100
    of steelworks, 95–8
    potential (defined), 98
Electric Furnace:
    costs of, 22–5